MIKE ROBERTSON

I SHOOK HANDS WITH
DEATH

MY EXPERIENCE COMING
FACE TO FACE WITH ETERNITY

Authentic

I Shook Hands with Death
Copyright © 2013
Mike Robertson

Cover design by Lookout Design, Inc.
Edited by W. Simon

Unless otherwise specified, Scripture quotations are taken from *The Holy Bible, New International Version*® NIV®. Copyright © 1973, 1978, 1984, 2011 by Biblica, Inc.™ Used by permission of Zondervan. All rights reserved worldwide. www.zondervan.com. The "NIV" and "New International Version" are trademarks registered in the United States Patent and Trademark Office by Biblica, Inc.™

Other versions used are:

AMP—Scripture quotations taken from the *Amplified*® *Bible,* Copyright © 1954, 1958, 1962, 1964, 1965, 1987 by The Lockman Foundation. Used by permission. (www.Lockman.org).

KJV—*King James Version,* Authorized King James Version.

NASB—Scripture taken from the *New American Standard Bible*®, Copyright © 1960, 1962, 1963, 1968, 1971, 1972, 1973, 1975, 1977, 1995 by The Lockman Foundation. Used by permission. (www.Lockman.org).

NKJV—Scripture taken from the *New King James Version.* Copyright © 1982 by Thomas Nelson, Inc. Used by permission. All rights reserved.

NLT—Scripture quotations marked (NLT) are taken from the *Holy Bible, New Living Translation,* copyright © 1996, 2004, 2007 by Tyndale House Foundation. Used by permission of Tyndale House Publishers, Inc., Carol Stream, Illinois 60188. All rights reserved.

Published by Authentic Publishers
188 Front Street, Suite 116-44
Franklin, TN 37064

Authentic Publishers is a division of
Authentic Media, Inc.

Library of Congress Cataloging-in-Publication Data

Robertson, Mike

    I Shook Hands with Death : My experience coming face to face
with eternity / Mike Robertson
    p. cm.

ISBN 978-1-78078-110-5
    978-1-78078-210-2 (e-book)

Printed in the United States of America

21 20 19 18 17 16 15 14   12 11 10 9 8 7 6 5 4 3 2

I dedicate this to my best friend,
my wife, Karen.
Had she known me one month prior
to my near-death experience,
she would have never looked my way.
I'm thankful God changed me.

CONTENTS

THE THIN BORDERLINE

MOST STUDIES OF HUMAN EMOTION and psychology say that for most people, public speaking is their number one fear, while the fear of dying is second on the list. I suppose this means that if you are at a funeral, you are better off in the casket than doing the eulogy.

There are a variety of ways that people can overcome the fear of public speaking...take a college class, enroll in enrichment seminars, or just speak in front of people enough times until you get over the fright. But how does a person overcome the fear of dying?

Fear of dying has led to discussions about the afterlife and paranormal activity, too. Hollywood has been quick to capitalize on what people are talking about these days, and the creative heads have rolled out detective dramas that examine the dead, ghost whisperers, ghost hunters, and even an apocalyptic series involving half-dead zombies roaming the countryside.

If you think this fear and fascination with dying is limited to show creators and reporters you would be wrong. Today, there are modern-day survivalists stockpiling weapons, ammo, food and water in comfortable underground bunkers in preparation for the next global holocaust. These people are determined to beat death when the rest of the planet goes up in smoke.

The universal curiosity and fear over dying runs so deep in humans that celebrating and appeasing the dead is not uncommon. In the U.S. we celebrate Halloween and All Saints Day; in Mexico it is Los Dias de los Muertos; and, in Japan it is the Obon Festival. Some of us may laugh at the holiday costumes and preparing food for spirits, but there are many people who take it seriously.

As the pastor of a large church in Central California, I have a front row seat on a weekly basis as people slip off into eternity. I hear a variety of questions and statements from those who are about to enter the next life. They always ask, "Am I going to make it to heaven?" "I am so afraid of the unknown." "What will it be like in eternity?"

Truth be told, there is a thin borderline separating this world and the next. I have met men and women who, as the end draws near, do not fear death—they actually welcome it. They do not embrace death in a suicidal or morose way. They know they have lived their lives well and look forward to meeting their

Maker. On the other hand, most people face dying with a measure of genuine anxiety. They are afraid of the unknown.

The message of this book is that we can have confidence that God holds our hands as we enter eternity. I know...I have been through a near-death encounter, and my experience has filled me with hope. I wish I could place my experience in a syringe and give everyone a shot!

As I share my story, you will realize that when your time comes to meet God, you do not need to fear dying. As you read this book, my hope and prayer is that you will understand that God created all of us and gave us a certain number of days on this earth. His ultimate goal, however, is that we will spend all eternity with Him in heaven, and I would like to help you to be prepared.

Let's start with day I shook hands with death.

THE DAY I SHOOK HANDS WITH DEATH

THIS IS IT—*the last day of my life!*

I can't believe what I am seeing. My body has hit the bottom of the lake and here I sit. I have the best seat in the house. Somehow, I am suspended about 50-feet above my body. I can see my body, but I'm not in it.

It happened too quickly. I didn't get to say goodbye to anyone. The only one or thing to say goodbye to is my lifeless corpse sitting in the dark, cold silt, 200-feet below the surface of an East Texas lake. "Goodbye, ole friend," I whisper.

I hover above my lifeless form. "I had fun living inside of you, but today I am being taken somewhere else."

These are the words I uttered to myself the day I shook hands with death. Before I get to my personal story in chapter three, however, let me offer a few thoughts on the subject of death, heaven, and the afterlife...

***

"The fear of death follows

from the fear of life.

A man who lives fully

is prepared to die at any time."

MARK TWAIN,
AMERICAN ADVENTURER, WRITER, 1835-1910

CHAPTER 1

WHY CHRISTIANS DIE BETTER (OR DO THEY?)

BEFORE I TELL YOU the rest of my near-death story at the bottom of a Texas lake, I want to share a bit about my father, as well as other truths about the afterlife. The day my Dad died was the genesis of much of my fascination with death, reading obituaries, and taking note of graveyards and headstones. On that day, I witnessed him speaking to people on the other side. It was so hard to comprehend in my youth. Did my dad really speak to dead people prior to his passing? I know that I am not a 'lone ranger' in my fascination with dying. People are naturally curious about what lies beyond our physical reality.

Having officiated over more funerals than I can count, I have dealt with my share of questions about what is on the other side. A lot of people look for answers during that time more than any other time of their lives. I have to confess, I have not always had the answer for all of the questions along the way. For example, the first funeral I ever performed was for a person who committed suicide while his companion was attending Sunday School. How do you console someone when a tragedy like that happens? How do you console the family of a man who murdered his two small children? What do you say to godly parents whose three-year-old child drowns in the babysitter's swimming pool? What sense can you make of that? Death seems especially hard when children and young people are facing it. There is a feeling that this person has been cheated out of a life that seems to have departed long before any reasonable expiration date. There is little comfort anyone can give in times like these.

You would think dying and death is easier for believers who have placed their trust in God who has prepared a place for them in the afterlife. However, I am not sure there is much difference between those who believe and those who profess no belief at all. This may be a shocking statement to those who follow Christ, but hear me out.

I believe the problem lies with the fact that we dwell on the aspect of death more than we do life. Death is so unnatural. When God created us, we were never meant to die. The shortest verse in the Bible will lend itself to that theory: "Jesus wept."

Jesus was weeping for His good friend Lazarus who had died. Jesus had completely entered into the human condition of grieving, but why? Why would the Son of God who knew more about the afterlife than anyone who has ever lived, weep?

Perhaps Jesus was lamenting over the pain Lazarus' sisters were experiencing. Or, perhaps Jesus knew what Lazarus was experiencing in the afterlife for four days, and He was about to bring Lazarus back to a less desirable place. Or, could it be that Jesus was weeping over the memories that He, Lazarus and the sisters had experi-

Since Jesus was every bit as human as you and me, the emotions He felt were akin to what we feel when someone we love has passed away.

enced. Memories do not have a "trickling in" effect at death, rather they explode on the scene like a fire hydrant whose valve has just been opened as far as it can—our mind is instantly flooded!

Even though we do not have an explanation afforded us in Scripture, let us theorize that it was the sweet memories He had of His friend that caused Jesus to weep. If I were to ask you, "When was the last time you had dined in a nice restaurant?" What would you say? Like everyone else you would have to think for a moment but almost all of us could recall the memory. Where did that memory come from? You were not thinking about that memory until I asked you to recall it. Death has a way of pulling memories to the frontal lobe of our thinking. Since Jesus was every bit as human as you and me, the emotions He felt were akin to what we feel when someone we love has passed away.

ARE WE DYING OR LIVING?

This year we are experiencing an invasion of the cicada bug. Every 17 years America has the privilege of hearing the very unique sound that only the cicada can make. When the temperature of the ground reaches a favorable point millions and millions of these little guys will pop up and make their way to a tree or an old worn out tire. There they will live until they shed their outer crust. Afterwards, they get on with providing us with their melodious tunes. They cannot sing until they shed the old.

In one of my talks, I display photos of myself that span my lifetime. The first photo is when I am about nine months old, in the next I am a teenager, then a college photo, and finally something recent. I then ask the audience which of the photos represents who I am. While myriad answers surface, the fact of the matter is, I am not any of those persons of the past. Medical science will tell you that you are dying each day. Like the cicada, we are shedding the old and replacing it with the new. Every molecule I had when I was a baby or even a teen has long gone.

So the question remains: am I living or am I dying? In order for us to live we have to die. Before we were born, we began dying. Had we not left some matters behind in the womb we would never be born. In life, we are constantly giving birth to our new self; we shed the old and give birth to what is new... that is true physically, mentally and spiritually. Jesus said it best, "unless a grain of wheat falls into the ground and dies, it remains alone; but if it dies, it produces much grain" (John 12:24, *NKJV*). He hit the nail right on the head. Now contrast that with Jesus' early statement to Lazarus' sister: "And whoever lives and believes in Me shall never die. Do you believe this?" (John 11:26, *NKJV*). It is liberating when we see death as a part of living.

Why is it then that we struggle so much when a loved one passes? It has to do with the past and certainly not the future. Even though Christians have invested their lives in the belief of the afterlife, very few are throwing parties in expectation of that day. We all want to go to heaven but who wants to die getting there? Entering into a phase of existence that we cannot control is more than the mind can comprehend. This is the final exam and none of us have studied much about it. Death is the final act of giving up total control; and giving up any measure of control has always been a battle for each of us.

MEMORIES

In the movie, *The Legend of Bagger Vance,* Matt Damon plays the character and depicts the life of Rannulph Junuh who returns from World War I with posttraumatic war syndrome. Today it is called "posttraumatic stress disorder" but the characteristics are the same. Symptoms develop in a person after direct experience from an extremely traumatic stressor like the threat of violent death or serious injury. Many of our brave soldiers who have seen horrors on the battlefield suffer from this when they return home and try to resume their prewar days. In the case of Bagger, there is a moment where he is inebriated with his poker-playing buddies. He then philosophies about how drunk is drunk enough? His explanation is remarkably true: "The answer is, it's all a matter of brain cells. Every drink of liquor you take kills brain cells. But that don't matter, you got billions more. First the sadness cells die, so you smile real big. Then the quiet cells go, so you talk real loud for no reason at all. That's okay, because the stupid cells go next, then everything you say is real smart. And finally...come the memory cells. Those are the toughest ones to kill."

We all want to go to heaven but who wants to die getting there? Entering into a phase of existence that we cannot control is more than the mind can comprehend.

Memories are what haunt most of us. We all could have done better in life and we all have those regrets unless we have dealt with them. While our bodies are wasting away one thing remains...those killer memories. Why is dying so hard? The answer: the vivid recall of past events (memories) where we see the loved one's face or recall some powerful verbal exchange taunts us to re-evaluate and re-experience our relationship with that deceased person. When we ask a question, we awaken those memories...we unlock all the emotions that give that memory substance. Thousands of our memories are like that—hidden away—until awakened by a question. Give any of us a moment and we can retrieve a host of memories.

I contend that memories make dying a hard experience for us. When death invades the ranks of our brain cells, memories have a way of taking a front-row seat in our thinking. If it were not for the memories, grieving would not be grieving. Think about standing at a coffin of a departed one...our minds are in memory mode. When you bring a memory to mind, you are investing your emotions—joy, sorrow, elation and heartache—in that memory. What also makes it difficult is all the unfinished business we believe we have in connection with that person. We are kicking ourselves over the kind words we never said, the harsh words we did say, or things we wanted to accomplish. And the worst of all feelings—regret. May God help us to live out our days without regrets.

We make death an almost unbearable experience, because we are in memory mode and not in living mode. One of the great thrills of having children around is the delight of watching them experience things for the first time. Watch a child as they experience Disney World for the first time. What a day of delight! They witness the magnificent display of fireworks at Disney World. They are awestruck. Compare that day to their fourth, fifth or sixth time visiting Disney World. The thrill is not what it used to be—Mickey has lost his mojo; the mouse does not have his magic like before. Repetition has settled in and you know just about everything that is going to happen. Disney is the same but you are not the same. Jesus said, "unless you change and become like little children, you will never enter the kingdom of heaven" (Matthew 18:3).

The Bible also says that God's compassion for us is new every morning (see Lamentations 3:22). Think about it. God is so creative that we are going to be in heaven for tens of thousands of years and still be in discovery mode. Imagine, if He wanted to, He could wipe out everything we experienced yesterday and give us a brand new experience every day. Our focus is best served when we dwell on living rather than dying. Some wise person said years ago: "Our dreams must be bigger than our memories."

GIVING OVER CONTROL

As we age, our desires change drastically. Compare the desires of a 16-year-old teenager to a 96-year-old senior and you would not find many similarities! The young have yet to amass experiences while the older have little energy left to enjoy many experiences. The energy it takes to enjoy the things we did in our youth is not there. Sitting in a La-Z-Boy chair and taking a nap is much more exciting than going for a joy ride around town. The elderly have had time to work on many things and eventually realize that there are some things they cannot do anymore. They have come to terms that someone else is in charge.

There is a great deal of maturity that comes from knowing what you can and cannot do because your body is not what it used to be. The quicker we can give up control then the sooner peace will equip our hearts and minds. The secret is letting go on the inside. You say to yourself: "I no longer have control. Better yet, I no longer care to have control!" Death is the final act of surrendering all control.

HELPING THE DYING DIE

Letting go may be the most difficult thing any of us do. I remember how I was fascinated by the stories of a nurse performing hospice care. Hospices focus on the care of a terminally ill patient while also attending to the patient's emotional and spiritual needs. It confirmed my belief that people of faith handle dying better than those individuals who do not carry any hope of an afterlife. Death is the amplification of what each of us is confronted with all of our lives—*surrendering.* I grew up listening to the famous evangelist Billy Graham on television. One of his favorite songs to play at decision time was *I Surrender All.* Doesn't that pretty much sum it up? The earlier we learn how to surrender ourselves the better life goes for us. Hence, if we have never practiced the art of surrender then no doubt dying is going to be the most difficult thing we ever do. Not only is it the final act of giving up control, it is the ultimate act of surrendering.

> *The earlier we learn how to surrender ourselves the better life goes for us.*

The secret to it all has to be down deep on the inside of each of us. When we find God and accept Jesus Christ into our life, we are equipped with a peace that Paul talks about in Philippians 4:7: "And the peace of God, which transcends all understanding, will guard your hearts and your minds in Christ Jesus." The anxiety that comes with dying when facing the unknown is not the predominant factor that a Christian feels (or should feel) at the end of his or her life. Fear and anxiety have been replaced with faith that there is a God, and there is life beyond death! Since I have come to understand that reality, I know everything is going to be all right. While I am unable to explain all that may await this transitional time of our lives, I have surrendered to the fact that I am leaving this dimension and moving onto the next. I think this is the key.

As Jesus said to Martha, "I am the resurrection and the life. He who believes in Me, though he may die, he shall live" (John 11:25 *NKJV*). I am leaving my earthly life and accepting my life in eternity. I am leaving this body for my new heavenly form. No doubt this is why the elderly die better than the young. In speaking with my nurse friend who provides hospice care, she has witnessed hundreds passing over into the next dimension, she says that dying is especially difficult for the young. They did not get a chance to live and have not become tired of their earthly shell. The elderly on the other hand have grown tired of their old creaky body that increasingly requires more and more maintenance.

BELIEVER ASSISTED DYING

My mom was 95 when she departed. She placed her faith in Jesus Christ while she was a teen. She did her best to raise eight children with the love of God. I had the privilege to visit her each weekend before her passing. In her final days, she was heavily medicated and that affected her outlook on life. I did my best, along with my siblings, to encourage her and give her reassurance.

I discovered that if we shift a person's focus away from the questions: "Why and how this is happening to me?" I think we can greatly assist them passing over. The first thing I and my siblings did was to share with mom about the good times. She had lived a beautiful life. We chose to focus on those beautiful moments rather than all the things that went wrong. I would often tell her, "Mom you ought to be proud of what you have done. Your children all love God and they are still talking to each other. You taught us how to love others and how to put others first. You taught us how to be givers." She had the gift of giving. (When speaking to one who is heavily medicated, recalling positive things and good times in their life has to be reiterated.)

The next thing my family did was to raise questions and discussions about what mom was really giving up. If you have a loved one with a tired body, you can gently point and encourage them that they have a new one in the Lord. Hardly anyone who has made peace with God would choose this old worn out body over getting a new model. Surrendering this tired body for a better one from God is like giving up a broken-down 1984 Gremlin with a vinyl interior and an AM radio/cassette for a brand new Maserati or Lexus with leather upholstery, a Bose sound system, and GPS map system.

One of the major things we also discussed with mom was the subject of regrets. I asked her, "Do you have any regrets?"

She could not think of any. "Do you feel like there is any unfinished business?" She felt there were some items that needed to be addressed. She wanted all her grandkids and great grandkids to make a decision to follow Christ. She felt that was the only thing she was leaving undone. I assured her that I would tell them, and I did at her funeral. To me, it is a no-brainer. If we want to see our loved ones again we have to make a decision to go where they are going.

ADDING VALUE TO LIFE BEFORE YOU EXIT

Jesus left us a great example of handling the bereaved. Before He died, He had a meal with His closest friends. He passed out bread and began to talk to them about His life and why He came to live on the earth. He was not handing out gold coins worth millions to be placed in their Jewish bank accounts or leaving them large estates in the countryside. He gave them something of much greater value. One of the great deceptions of life is when we focus on money and possessions rather than on things that really matter. Those who cannot wait for their loved ones to die, because they want to claim an inheritance have fumbled the ball. What a waste when it comes to our eternal salvation. Jesus said it best, "For what profit is it to a man if he gains the whole world, and loses his own soul? Or what will a man give in exchange of his soul?" (Matthew 16:26 *NKJV*)

Instead Jesus has communion with the disciples. I am a spiritual person and I understand that we are in a battle with fallen spirits that war against our souls. Those evil spirits are relentless. They hang out with the dying hoping to get some last-minute digs. One thing is for sure, evil spirits do not like communion. The elements of communion consist of bread and fruit from the vine (some churches use grape juice and others use wine). The bread represents the body of Christ and the juice His blood that was shed for our redemption. Each time we share in communion it is a memorial that remembers His suffering death, and a prophecy of His Second Coming. As a matter-of-fact it was at communion time with His disciples that Judas, "the betrayer," revealed his hand. Judas had made a deal with the authorities to disclose Jesus' whereabouts and arrange for the Lord's arrest.

The day Jesus was crucified by Roman authorities, He hung between two known robbers. One of the robbers cried out in pain and demanded that if Jesus were the Son of God that He save them. This guy did not understand that there is something more in life than pain. I like what someone said: "Pain is weakness leaving the body." This fellow cried out for relief from immediate, temporal pain.

The other thief wised up on his deathbed. To my knowledge, this is the only deathbed conversion in the Bible. He placed his thoughts not on temporal pain, but eternal pain. What a decision! Pastor Rick Warren says that life here on the earth is comparable to preschool. Our time on the earth is so short in comparison to eternity. Another way to think about it is if you have a yardstick, then life here would measure about 1/16th of our existence when compared to eternity.

Maybe the second thief is teaching us how to die. I remember years ago consoling the children of a godly lady who died. All of her children had gathered around her bed as she was taking her last breaths. One of her children commented, "Mom taught us how to live and now she has taught us how to die." She was a godly woman who had surrendered to death. She, along with the apostle Paul looked death square in the face and said, "O death, where is thy sting? O grave, where is thy victory?" (1 Corinthians 15:55, *KJV*).

Death may be alien to creation, but how to address death and dying should not be strange to us. The Bible has a lot to share about death and life. Its pages record near-death encounters, and how saints of old faced dying with courage and peace, and how the most stubborn of people came to be saved by God's mighty hand.

Death may be alien to creation, but how to address death and dying should not be strange to us.

And as my friend Rona Swanson puts it, "And soon, one day, death itself will be put to death, forever defeated and unable to wound any more. Until that time, we do not grieve as those who have no hope. Our bright hope is beyond the horizon at present, but the promise of that Day's dawning is sure."

PERSONAL QUEST

1. What are your fears about dying?

2. Is it good to grieve for the loss of a loved one? If so, how long? If not, why?

3. Can you let go of a painful memory involving someone who has died? If so, how?

4. How have you or would you assist someone dying?

5. Can feeling regret be constructive or is it ultimately destructive when someone you love is dying?

***

"Do not pray for easy lives.

Pray to be stronger men.

Do not pray for tasks equal

to your powers.

Pray for powers equal

to your tasks.

Then the doing of your

work will be no miracle,

but you shall be the miracle."

PHILLIPS BROOKS,
AMERICAN EPISCOPAL BISHOP, 1835–1893

CHAPTER 2

NEAR-DEATH EXPERIENCES IN THE BIBLE

IF YOU HAVE EVER SEEN the movie *Saving Private Ryan*, doubtless you remember the scene at the end of the film—Ryan is an elderly man visiting the Normandy American Cemetery and Memorial with his family in Normandy, France. He stands at the grave of Captain Miller who was instrumental in saving his life. It is an emotional scene as Ryan looks at the grave with tears in his eyes. He asks his wife to confirm that he has led a good life and that he is a "good man" and thus worthy of the sacrifice of Miller and the others. Ryan, decades removed from the rescue, still wonders if his life was worth saving. He then salutes Miller's grave.

There are times when I wonder why I survived my near-death experience (more on this shortly). Why was my life worth saving? The answer to this question resides in the heart of the Scriptures. The Bible records the lives of those who died or came close to dying a physical death only to be brought back to life—in some fashion all were miraculously saved. Each person was dramatically changed through a NDE (near death experience). Each fulfilled the assignment God gave him. What they learned and shared is important for living powerfully in God.

JONAH'S SECOND CHANCE

Most people do not like the thought of being eaten or swallowed by an animal. Go to your local zoo or watch a program on Animal Planet and observe the lions, crocodiles, and sharks—the big beasts. Trust me, you never want to be their next meal. Well, in the Bible that is what happened to a prophet named Jonah—he was delivered into the belly of a beast and delivered out of it.

In the Bible, Jonah had been told to preach repentance to the city of Nineveh which was inhabited by a ruthless people called the Assyrians. These "bad boys" had long been an enemy to Jonah and his people the Israelites. From Jonah's perspective, the thought that the people of Nineveh might humble themselves and repent was not what he wanted to hear. What Jonah wanted was their destruction...not their salvation. So Jonah caught the first ship going West because he had no intention of listening to God's call upon his life. It's funny, Jonah actually thought he could outrun God and be a "no show" on his responsibilities.

While at sea God stirred up a huge storm. Jonah knew he was rebelling against God's will. He told the people onboard that the storm was his fault for disobeying God, and that they could calm the sea by throwing him overboard. The crew, acting as judge, jury and executioner, decided to throw Jonah into the sea. Sure enough, the storm came to an end. Now you may think the sailors acted in haste. You may even think their actions were a bit harsh—many people do. However, I think they did the right thing. I believe too many people bail out a rebellious heart before that person receives the full benefit of chastening from God. C.S. Lewis said, "Pain plants the flag of reality in the fortress of a rebel's heart." Some people always try to rescue their kids from the consequences of a bad choice, but trouble is what heaven placed on the menu to get the prodigal back to God.

I often jest when speaking on the story of Jonah. Jonah was a dark-skinned man (many people of that day had a dark complexion), and God disciplined Jonah by allowing the whale to swallow him. Now let your imagination run a bit. I am convinced that when the whale spewed Jonah up and on to the beach that he came out bleached white! Having been in the belly of the whale for three days, he had been well marinated in gastric juices. It is hard not to laugh when you visualize the scene, but there is a serious side to the entire ordeal, too.

Regardless if you go along with my humor or not, you have to realize that being swallowed by an enormous creature from the deep sea was a very horrific experience for Jonah. How much closer could you get to dying than being cooped up in the belly of a 10-ton fish? He must have thought he was going to die multiple times or at least wished he had been killed.

When Jonah came out of that great mammal, and found himself sprawled out on the sandy shore, he did what he was supposed to have done a few weeks prior…he headed off to Nineveh. Jonah prayed quite a few powerful prayers while in that great behemoth of the sea. I believe Jonah ultimately told God that he would do what God had wanted from the outset and that is why he survived his near-death experience. Even though he hit a few more rough patches during his lifetime, Jonah ultimately completed his assignment on the earth.

THE LONGEST NDE IN THE BIBLE

Lazarus has the record for the longest running near-death experience in the Bible. The Bible talks about Lazarus and his sisters, Mary and Martha, as being close friends to Jesus. Every time Jesus would pass by the place where they lived, He would stop for a visit and often Jesus would eat a meal with them, too.

One day, Lazarus became very ill. Mary and Martha sent word to Jesus that Lazarus was sick because they knew the Lord could heal him. Yet, Jesus does something very strange. He does not rush to be by Lazarus' side—rather Jesus remains at His location for two more days!

The timetable here is interesting to note: Jesus' delay results in Lazarus dying. By the time He gets there, the body has been laid to rest for four days. According to old Jewish beliefs, the soul protests the body's death and lingers near the body for three days, hoping that it will return to life. After three days, the soul leaves. By being in the grave four days, no one could dispute that there was no life left in Lazarus. But Jesus had other plans. Jesus commanded the mourners gathered at the grave that day to take away the stone and spoke in a loud voice for Lazarus to come out of the tomb (see John 11). Something miraculous happened—Lazarus came out! Four days gone...three words from Jesus...two happy sisters...one life renewed.

We do not have much recorded about Lazarus after he came back. I am confident he fulfilled his duty on the earth since he was a close friend to Jesus. The story of Lazarus being raised from the dead is a life-altering lesson for us: Lazarus did not stay in the tomb. When Jesus removed the stone and called out to Lazarus...he came forth. Friend, what is the stone blocking you from a new life? Let Jesus take the stone away! Listen to His voice and live!

PAUL GETS STONED

In Acts, chapter 14, we are told how the Apostle Paul was preaching the Good News of Christ in Lystra. He was having great success—people were born again, healed and being discipled in the Lord. There was, however, a crowd that had come to Lystra from Antioch and Iconium where Paul had been previously preaching. They hated Paul for what he and his evangelist team had done in their city. They cleverly persuaded the people of Lystra that Paul was an evil man and should be stoned to death.

What a rock concert that was! Kill me any way you want but please do not kill me by stoning! If you have ever been hit in the head with a single rock, imagine what it would be like to be hit by rock after rock until you died. Paul was pummeled by rocks and left for dead outside the city, but the other disciples gathered around him. Determined to share the Good News, Paul rose up and went back into the city to the amazement of those who hated him.

If you have ever been hit in the head with a single rock, imagine what it would be like to be hit by rock after rock until you died.

Many years later Paul would write about his experience:

"I must go on boasting. Although there is nothing to be gained, I will go on to the visions and revelations from the Lord, I know a man in Christ who fourteen years ago was caught up to the third heaven. Whether it was in the body or out of the body I do not know—God knows. And I know that this man—whether in the body or apart from the body I do not know, but God knows—was caught up to paradise and heard inexpressible things, things that no one is permitted to tell" (2 Corinthians 12:1-4).

Paul stated not once, but twice "Whether in the body or apart from the body I do not know, but God knows…"

Paul was still pondering his near-death experience years after the event had passed. He was still struggling to convey what wonders he had seen. That is a common occurrence of those who have had a near-death experience. They come back with stories of things they saw or felt, and yet they are unable to fully explain some of the amazing things they encountered. Many describe colors or intense feelings, which have no point of reference here on the earth. Others can only say, "There are no words that I know of that can fully describe what I saw and felt…no words."

In the end, the most important question for any believer who has had a near-death experience—even Paul with his seeing paradise—is "What did you do with your life afterwards?" In Paul's case, he became a prolific writer; he authored over half the New Testament. If that is not enough, he had multiple missionary journeys throughout the Roman Empire as well. He was truly passionate to share how Christ had saved his life.

JOHN THE REVELATOR

If you will take some extra time to study the biblical account, you will find out that the authorities tried to kill John, but he would not die. Then, they banished him to the Isle of Patmos where John had a NDE. There, he was caught up in the spirit and shown heaven. His experience was so powerful and extensive that he wrote the entire Book of Revelation. John also authored four other writings that made their way into the New Testament. I think you would agree that John did something with his life upon returning to this world.

But it does not end there because John also records in Revelation, Chapter 11, two near-death experiences that will occur in the future. God is talking and states that during the Great Tribulation, "I will give power to my two witnesses..." (Revelation 11:3, *NLT*). Many people have speculated as to the identities of the two witnesses; I believe they are Elijah and Moses. God hid the body of Moses and there is not anyone who knows where it is but God. In Elijah's case, he was taken up into heaven in a chariot of fire. Regardless how these two men were taken, they will both come back because their work on earth is not completed. John's vision of humankind's future may be troubling to some, but the book is a great study on God's long-suffering heart, His judgment, mercy, and Second Coming.

JESUS DEFEATED DEATH

As Christians, we know Jesus died, was buried, and rose on the third day—it is the core of our faith. His resurrection over death is the great sign, the irrefutable credential, that Jesus is Lord of all.

When Jesus rose from the grave and before He ascended into the clouds, He spent a number of weeks on earth appearing before His disciples and closest friends. I am sure they had plenty of questions about His dying and His resurrection. His appearance to them was profound proof of an afterlife, but also proof of God's immeasurable love to send His only Son to die on our behalf, and to provide salvation to any who believed in His Name.

The Apostle Paul wrote, "But Christ has indeed been raised from the dead, the firstfruits of those who have fallen asleep. For since death came through a man, the resurrection of the dead comes also through a man" (1 Corinthians 15:20-21). Jesus not only experienced death and was restored to this world for a brief time, but He returned with an imperishable body that speaks of the world to come when the perishable gives way to the imperishable.

A NDE IGNITES PASSION TO SERVE CHRIST

I once listened to a businessman who gave his personal account of going to heaven and back. He was able to see the grandeur of heaven, but was forbidden entrance by Jesus Himself. He asked why he could not stay, and Jesus told him it was because he had not done enough on the earth. A discussion occurred between him and Jesus, and the Lord eventually asked him: "Can you think of anything you have done that warrants your entry into heaven?"

The businessman thought and thought, and then remembered how one day while in grade school, he walked some kids across a school crossing. That was all he could muster. In hearing the story I thought to myself, *Ooops! That's not going to help you much.* The man was in his 50s and all he could think about was something that happened at least four decades prior.

Let me pause here for a moment to make something very clear—*our works on earth do not gain us entry into heaven.* Only our faith in Jesus Christ and His substitute for our sins on the cross can get us into heaven. You get to go to heaven by your faith in Jesus Christ—nothing more and nothing less. Having said that…you need to understand that good works do play a part once we get to heaven. We will be judged according to our works. "For we must all appear before the judgment seat of Christ, so that each of us may receive what is due us for the things done while in the body, whether good or bad" (2 Corinthians 5:10).

After some time, I heard from this businessman again. He still had not done anything noteworthy with his life! I wanted to yell at him and tell him he needed a "checkup from the neck up!" He finished his testimony like this: "I am still looking for something to do. I think I will find it someday." How awful and painful an admission—a waste of a second chance at life! Do not let that happen to you.

Let me pause here for a moment to make something very clear— our works on earth do not gain us entry into heaven.

I don't know what you think about the local church but it is the best place to give something back to the Lord with the time you have on earth. If you are not a person who attends a church, I would encourage you to find one that is exciting and believes the whole Bible and is not afraid to pray for the sick or to worship God. Pastor Bill Hybels says: "The local church is the hope of the world." I firmly believe that is true. Any kind of investment you make in the right local church will ring through the annals of eternity and you will be greeted by a great reward on the other side.

Many years ago my near-death experience radically altered my direction and perception of life and in serving Christ. I was the most reckless of rebels in my youth. I was drowning physically, emotionally, and spiritually. But then God interrupted my life. He literally reached out and rescued me. God's amazing grace helped me to love the lost, the Church, and Him. God gave me a second chance!

Let me share my story with you.

PERSONAL QUEST

1.   What are some common characteristics that near-death experience (NDE) survivors share in what they have seen and observed on the other side that you have heard or read about?

2.   Why is the discussion about people returning from a NDE of popular interest today?

3.   If a NDE is not required for a person to repent and be saved, why does God allow some people to have a NDE?

4.   Could the devil use a NDE to hinder a person from believing in Christ?

5.   If you have or did go through a NDE, what in this world would draw you back? Why?

* * *

"Pride is a spiritual cancer:

it eats up the very

possibility of love,

or contentment,

or even common sense."

C.S. LEWIS,
BRITISH PROFESSOR, WRITER, AND CHRISTIAN
APOLOGIST, 1898–1963

CHAPTER 3

THE GREAT LIFEGUARD

THIS IS IT—THE LAST DAY OF MY LIFE!

I can't believe what I am seeing. My body has hit the bottom of the lake and here I sit. I have the best seat in the house. Somehow, I am suspended about 50-feet above my body. I can see my body, but I'm not in it.

It happened too quickly. I didn't get to say goodbye to anyone. The only one or thing to say goodbye to is my lifeless corpse sitting in the dark, cold silt, 200-feet below the surface of an East Texas lake. "Goodbye, ole friend," I whisper.

I hover above my lifeless form. "I had fun living inside of you, but today I am being taken somewhere else."

✳✳✳

Those were my thoughts the day I died...a warm August day two weeks before my 20th birthday. But we need to hit the rewind button first...you need to know how I arrived at the lake. It wasn't by accident...nothing is by accident.

I grew up in Littlefield, West Texas. The population was around 7,000 growing up. It was a small town—think "Mayberry RFD," Superman's "Smallville," the Hobbit's "Shire." Our big claim to fame is that it is the hometown of country singer Waylon Jennings. I played football with his son, Terry. He was the quarterback, and I was the tight end. You didn't have to lock your doors because everybody felt safe. Kids walked miles to school and never had to worry about being abducted by strangers.

It's kind of funny looking back on it... we were so poor that even thieves brought what they stole to our house.

My dad seemed to step right out of the Old Testament. The Robertson clan was a large family with three boys and five girls. We were poor but never realized how poor. It's kind of funny looking back on it...we were so poor that even thieves brought what they stole to our house.

When I was a little boy, Mom and Dad took me (usually kicking and screaming) to a little Baptist church on Sundays. I often joke with people saying that my mom had a drug problem because she often "drug" me to church given all my protests to be somewhere else. She often told me, "You're going to go into the ministry one day, Michael D."

"No way, Mom," I'd reply. "Preachers are poor. I don't want to be poor. Besides, God can't afford me." I was stubborn. I had grown up seeing ministers drive old cars, wear second-hand clothes, and being fed with food from other folks. That was not the life for me! No way! I wanted more than that.

I was a typical teenager looking for something—but I didn't know what it was. I had a constant nagging feeling that I was born for a special purpose, something greater than I could imagine, but it eluded me. It wasn't long before I found myself experimenting with drugs and alcohol—not to excess, but just enough to help fill the void in my life. I didn't know how to handle that nagging feeling other than to dull it with drugs and alcohol. I was restless, foolish…proud.

DEATH OF A DEAR FRIEND

When I was 16, my passion was fast muscle cars. It was in the family blood. My brother Johnny enjoyed racing cars, and he had plenty of friends who loved the competition. I eventually decided to buy a 1970 Dodge Super Bee. It was a two-door coupe wonder. Randal, the previous owner, told me to be careful with it. He had gotten it up to 161 mph. It had heavy-duty suspension, high-performance tires and a stripe (with the bee logo) wrapped around the tail. Oh, and inside…it was a race car with a sophisticated gauge and speedometer dash cluster. Sweet! I looked cool in it. Boy was I itchin' to see if I could break Randal's mile-per-hour record!

I may not have been the smartest guy in town, but no one could out-run me in the Super Bee. I would race anyone at any time. Some saw me as one of the "party guys" in town. People knew I liked to get high; I had an "attitude." The bumper sticker on the back of my sweet Super Bee read: "National Gun Week, Let's Get Loaded!" You can imagine…I was a police magnet.

When I hit age 17, you could say I was "an accident waiting to happen." In August of that year, my friends and I were up to the usual activities: getting high, listening to rock-n-roll, and congregating around a 16-gallon keg of beer. We were all at the caliche pit outside of town when my friend Michael Cotter said, "Let's go to town and drag Main." Not really having anything else better to do, we all just shrugged and said, "Why not!"

We jumped up, stumbled over to the Super Bee, hopped in and headed down the highway. In the car, Michael then threw out a challenge to me, "Let's see how fast we can go." I was so familiar with the road, I knew if we could get it to 100 mph by a certain point, I could coast all the way onto Main Street. And that's exactly what we did.

I drove the Super Bee to 100 mph and put it in neutral to coast the final stretch. I was still doing 70 mph when we drove in front of the high school. It was then that I noticed a vehicle about one-quarter mile ahead in our lane. The car was idling as someone was conversing with someone else on a front porch. I thought, *This is not good.*

I hit the brakes, but at 70 mph the brakes began to lock up. To miss the car ahead, I turned the wheel and began to maneuver into the lane of the on-coming traffic. After skidding a couple hundred feet, I came in contact with the on-coming traffic. The Super Bee was about to be T-boned.

The smell of burning rubber filled my senses as the screeching tires left their dark black marks on the road...the sound of metal hitting metal as the passenger side of the car folded like an accordion. I was overcome by the deafening screams of Michael as he was hit by the on-coming traffic, pinning him in the car. I fell out the driver's side unharmed but badly shaken.

It was the worst night of my life.

Looking back now, I think "How could I have been so dumb!" But at 17, the frontal lobe of your brain (where you make wise decisions) is not fully developed. That is why young people are the greatest risk takers—their brain is not equipped to calculate the severity of a bad decision. For a growing teenager, exercising independence, resisting and rejecting advice from those who are older was the way to go. We were invincible; we knew what we could do; we weren't afraid because we never thought about consequences.

After the accident, Michael spent weeks in intensive care at the hospital. He had so many broken bones; his pelvis had been crushed, too. Michael was a pretty good athlete and a great pole-vaulter. Some of his coaches and town residents had felt that he could have become a contender in the state pole-vaulting championships. But now that hope and dream was shattered because of my stupidity. It was my fault. Mike was paying the consequences of my monumental, bad idea to drive while drunk.

When Michael got out of the hospital, I carried and drove him around town. I had to borrow my Dad's cherry red Chevy truck since the Super Bee was totaled. I would place Michael's wheelchair in the back of the truck, and get him in and out of places. I was trying to make up for the awful thing I had done to him and his family.

Meanwhile, the authorities were pressing charges: attempted vehicular manslaughter. The only person who saved me was Michael's mom. When the police approached her family about pressing charges, she said, "No! It could have been my son behind the wheel driving that car just as much as it was Thelma's son." Mrs. Cotter saved my life that day—and I got the first of several undeserved second chances. I have never been able to repay the damage I did to Mike, his mom, and the Cotter family. But since she was not willing to press charges, I got off with a DUI and probation.

Now you'd think that I had gotten my act together at this point—right? Wrong. I was feeling so miserable over the accident involving Michael that I plunged myself into the party scene. I had to numb the pain.

DUMB AND DUMBER

By December, we were about to have exams and then go into the Christmas break from school. One day, I was planning to head home and study for the exam, but my friends offered me the opportunity to party and get high with them. We were driving around town and having way too much fun. Of course, we got pulled over by the police. The smell of marijuana is very distinct and as I watched the policeman walk toward the car, I knew what would come next. We were arrested. After spending the night in jail, I knew I was in big trouble. I was already on probation.

Believe me you don't ever want to go to jail in the wintertime in West Texas. I was placed in the city hall jail. My friend had been there the week before. He was so angry about being locked up that he broke out the windows and tried to flush the bed quilts down the toilet. Yuck! Can you imagine…here I am, a 17-year-old guy in a jail cell with broken windows, the wind whipping through the frigid cell, with nothing—absolutely nothing to wrap myself up in. And I'm scared…there are other guys here in the jail. I remember thinking, *When I get out of here, I am never coming back!* I was released the next day and you can't imagine how much distance I put between myself and that jail. Even after all these years I still cannot forget the experience…jail is one place you never want to be.

When I returned to my high school, the administration decided that they no longer needed my services—they suspended me. They had a rule that anyone arrested on drug-related charges would be suspended; I was forbidden to take the quarterly exams. Credits for that quarter would also be forfeited. Basically, they said, you can't finish this quarter and since you can't take the exams, you'll simply have to return next year to finish. I was full of pride and it was beginning to cost me dearly. I knew "next year" meant I'd be with a bunch of underclassmen. I thought, *Forget this!* It was my last day in high school. Being the cool person I was, I decided that as soon as possible I would take the GED exam (high school equivalency), which was nine months later.

When I appeared in court for the possession of marijuana, the judge gave me a break. I received a charge of marijuana possession while under probation of a DUI. The judge said something I will never forget: "If I give you a chance, will you do something with your life?" I said, "I will." Yet at that time, I didn't really know what I was agreeing to. It was another undeserved second chance.

MY FASCINATION WITH OBITS

From a young age, death fascinated me—how people died and what they went through in the dying experience. Call it morbid curiosity, but the obituary page of the newspaper was always the first page I read every day. In the obits, the age of the people who died particularly interested me. When my friend Gary died at 17, I realized that being young does not give you a pass to live to old age. When it came to old people…well, it was natural for them to get worn out and to die. I had a simple way of lookin' at death. It was a view about to be shattered.

In February, the unthinkable occurred. I was drinking with my friend Brad in my parent's living room and watching TV when my Dad had a stroke. My father was a strong man and liked to get into fights when he was younger, but suddenly the stroke left him weak and fragile. Instantly, all of my curiosity about death and dying was staring me right in the face! Dad looked peaceful even though he was suffering excruciating pain and wasn't able to speak. There was a deep sense of calm that surrounded him.

I watched him slip in and out of consciousness. His lips sometimes moved as if he were having a conversation with someone. I would look at my family, my brothers and sisters who were surrounding him. They weren't talking to him, so who was Dad talking to? Every once in a while, Dad would smile and whisper a name. "Whose name did he say?" I asked.

"Meral," my brother answered. Meral was my dad's sister who had died a long time ago.

"C-c-c-can't be," I stuttered. "She's dead. You don't think he can really see her do you?"

Time and time again, the same thing happened...another smile...another name whispered. We were in awe of what we were witnessing. Who did he see? What was he experiencing? Whatever or whoever it was, it gave him a strong sense of assurance. He just looked so peaceful. Suddenly, his eyes opened wide with wonder, and he looked straight at my brother, Johnny. As Johnny leaned in close, my father whispered in a low raspy voice, "Death has no sting." He then closed his eyes and was gone from this world.

My mind was reeling from my father's passing but also in the way it happened. My dad had conversations with people who had died! I thought, *No way!* Grief stricken and blaming God for taking my father, I coped the only way I knew how—I got high. After that day, I started sinking further and further into a hole of despair and self-destruction. I was a 17-year-old dropout in charge of my late father's nursery, his grocery store, and a trucking business. Within months, I managed those businesses into failure. I had to get a job just to help my mom and sisters survive.

MAKING ENDS MEET

When I turned 18, I began to work in the oil fields to help Mom pay the bills. Finances were tight after Dad died. Working in the oil fields wasn't easy, but I wasn't afraid of hard work. I worked harder than anyone around me as a deck hand, and I was making pretty good money. I knew if I could get promoted to the tower deck, that's where I could make the real money, and I wouldn't have to get as dirty as I did working on the floor. My bosses didn't seem to appreciate my effort, though. They refused to promote me, so I quit. At least, that was the excuse I came up with. The real reason I left that job was that I had to work in a dried up riverbed in a snowstorm on Christmas Eve. I hated that! After I quit, I wondered, *What am I going to do next? Why am I on the earth in the first place?*

Years before, Dad had operated a grocery store. In my early teens, he had sat me down and told me that the grocery business was a good career choice for me. He convinced me when he said, "People will always have to eat."

That's it, I thought. *That's real job security.*

I was 19 when I received a call from the owner of the local supermarket. I had worked for Furr's Supermarket in the past. When he called, he said he had a job for me stocking shelves at 50 cents an hour less than I was making in the oil fields, but I took it. Fifty cents less to work in an air-conditioned building and not get your clothes dirty—now that was the job for me. Plus, I'd get to see a lot of pretty girls. I knew from previous experience that girls often shopped with their moms.

Again, I was a good employee and worked my way up the pay scale, but I didn't get the position I felt I deserved. I wanted to be the store manager, but they wouldn't promote me. I kept on working, but I knew I was born for more. Little did I know at the time that the Lord had plans for me. He wasn't allowing me to be content and successful.

I was working the afternoon/evening shift, grumbling to myself about missing another night out with my friends, when my eyes beheld a particularly attractive girl. I'd seen her around town a few times. She was close to my age, but when she walked in that night, there was something different about her.

She walked up to me with an angelic smile. She spoke softly, "I'd like to invite you to come to the Assemblies of God church for a special service. I know God wants to fill the emptiness that's inside you."

What? How did she know what I was feeling? I asked her if any girls were going to be there. She said that there would be plenty of girls. That's what sold me. She didn't need to say anything more—I knew I would probably go so I could check out all the pretty girls. She purchased the few items she came in for and then left. But her invitation lingered in my mind.

I was very curious, so I decided to go to the church after my shift. My life had already hit rock bottom and I thought, *What do I have to lose?*

In the middle of the meeting, they had what they called a "prayer time." The preacher asked if they could pray for me, but I didn't know what that meant in an Assemblies of God church. About 20 young people gathered around me and began to pray aloud. I thought it was a little strange, but it didn't bother me that much. The more they prayed, the better I felt. After a few minutes went by, they quit praying, and I was born again!

Something incredible happened that night. I walked out on the porch and realized that my desires had immediately changed.

Something incredible happened that night. I walked out on the porch and realized that my desires had immediately changed. I looked up at the stars and couldn't believe how bright they were. I immediately had an appreciation of God that I'd never imagined before. Many of my self-defeating habits were suddenly gone. I just didn't have the desire to do what I used to do to try to fill the nagging emptiness in my heart. The emptiness had been filled with God's grace.

As I started reading my Bible, I discovered this is what the New Testament referred to as being Spirit-filled. In his letter to the Ephesians, Paul wrote, "Do not get drunk on wine, which leads to debauchery. Instead, be filled with the Spirit" (Ephesians 5:18).

That night I called my brother Terry on the phone and woke him up. He and many others had been praying for my salvation. (This is an important lesson for all of us: Don't ever stop praying for lost loved ones. Prayer is the most powerful tool in the salvation of others.) When I told him I'd been born again, Terry was not sure if he believed me. Many times before, he had heard me say I was straightening up my life. That night, I could not convince him over the phone that I had really changed, but I knew that a power had come into me, and that power was making me the person God wanted me to be.

Even though Terry did not believe it at first, the change was real. For the next month, my family saw that a genuine transformation had taken place in my life, and they were amazed. No more smoking, partying, drinking or getting high. I knew my family had been praying for me, and Mom was thrilled to see her prayers answered.

GOD LIFEGUARDING ME

A month later, in August, we had a family reunion at Lake O' the Pines, which is located in the pine-filled woods of East Texas. The large lake was a beautiful setting to get together with the family. I was eager to see my brothers and sisters who had moved away from home.

My brother Johnny and I were excited to be there. After we'd been there for a while talking and laughing with our extended family, Johnny and I decided to take a canoe out on the lake. We wanted to see how long it would take us to paddle to the other side. I don't know if it was the excitement of being together or the "macho-ness" of the challenge, but we jumped in the canoe and started to paddle, leaving our life jackets lying on the beach.

It was a beautiful, sunny Texas day. Johnny and I raced across the water. By the time we got to the middle of the lake, we were about 200 yards from the shore. With our paddles, we both reached into the water at the same time on the right side of the canoe, and to our surprise, the canoe capsized! As I fell out of the canoe, I yelled at the top of my lungs, "Jesus, save me!"

I plunged into the water, and the canoe flipped over and hit me in the head. Feeling a little dizzy, I reached for the canoe to try to steady myself to keep from sinking. At the same time, Johnny, who was also in the water on the other side of the canoe, reached for the canoe a little more quickly than me. As he flipped it over, the edge of the canoe hit me in the face, broke my nose and knocked me semi-conscious. I had no ability to keep myself afloat. I began to sink into the dark abyss of the lake.

Barely conscious, I knew my lungs were filling up with water. I instantly thought: *This is going to be the last day of my life.* We were far out on the lake, and no one could see us. Even if they had seen the canoe flip over, they wouldn't be able to get to me in time. I didn't know if Johnny even knew I was sinking.

As I inhaled for the last time, water filled my lungs, and the strangest sensation came over me. I could feel myself separate from my body. As I felt myself going up, I was looking at my lifeless, limp body sinking down into the murky water at the bottom of the lake. I watched until it came to rest at the bottom of the lake. Lake O' the Pines is over 200 feet deep in some places, and as my body hit the dirt and sand, a cloud of silt swirled around it in the water. At that moment, I knew...*I was dead.*

The water began to take on a new, startling appearance. The brightest light I'd ever seen enveloped the lake. It wasn't just something I saw—it was something I could strongly feel. A sense of overwhelming love filled me. All I wanted was to get inside the light. If I could just get to the light, I knew I'd be okay. All the fear I'd ever felt about dying was replaced by a strong, sudden attraction to the light. The most intense love, peace, and calm I'd ever imagined came from this wondrous light.

I experienced things that day that have been a part of my life ever since. I had never felt love like that before. My family had loved me. My girlfriend, Becky, had loved me. But I had never had the feeling of such a complete, unconditional love like I felt at that moment. All I wanted to do at that point was to explore the love and light. I felt like I was being lifted out of the water and into that love-filled light. It was like nothing I'd ever experienced, I was drawn to the light.

Words fail me at this point to completely describe what I was feeling. All I can say is that my sins had no place there. Sin was not an issue. Before this time, I always thought that when I met God, He would want to spend a lot of time talking about all the bad things I had done over my life. Wrong! It wasn't even an issue. I learned a powerful lesson in that moment: God's love covers a multitude of sins.

Even though I had been on the bottom of the lake for at least five minutes, time was unimportant. I enjoyed being inside the light, basking in the complete love and joy I was feeling. Then slowly, I noticed the light was fading. I could now see that there were two individuals swimming to the bottom of the lake. They reached my body and began carrying me toward the surface. I strained to see their faces, but I couldn't see them clearly. Who were they? As they carried me closer to the surface of the water, the light became dimmer until it was completely gone. I was having a near-death experience.

When the two men brought me to the surface of the water, the lake was buzzing with boats. In those few minutes since the accident, word had gotten to the shore that I was at the bottom of the lake. When my body broke the surface of the water, I was aware that I was no longer observing my body—I was back inside it. My body ached with pain each time I gasped for air, and water spewed out of my mouth. I could hear sounds and people around me, but I couldn't see them. At that moment, I was blind.

I called out, "Who saved me? Who got me out of the water?" But no one could tell me.

Gradually, I began to regain consciousness. My head was pounding as I was taken to shore. Still unable to see, I called out, "Who saved me? Who got me out of the water?" But no one could tell me. To this day, no one has been able to tell me anything about the two men who pulled me from the lake, where they came from, what they looked like, or where they went once I was safe. I don't know if they were human or not, but whoever they were, I'm greatly indebted to them.

After a few minutes on shore, I was still dazed and incoherent. I have been told by doctors that when a person is in a coma, it is important to have friends and family members speak to that person. Hearing a familiar voice helps them return to consciousness. These doctors explained, "People in a coma may not be able to respond, but they can hear you." My family cried and prayed over me as I lay on the shore. Actually, that was quite an enjoyable experience. They said they loved me and apologized for all the bad things they'd ever done to me. So I know it's true: People really do hear you talking to them when they are in a coma. As they talked to me, my mind began to clear. Finally, I was awake and alert.

The next day, my head was still pounding, but my sight had returned. As I lay in bed thinking about the previous 24 hours, I was in awe at the wonder and grace of God. I'd only been a born-again Christian for a month, and now I truly felt like I'd literally been born again! I had been given a second chance at life. Inside, I was asking God a lot of questions: *God, why did You take me through that experience? Lord, why did You put my family through the pain of not knowing whether I would live or die? Why God? Why?*

I was about to get an answer.

PERSONAL QUEST

1. How does God protect a person from their
   destructive tendencies and behaviors?

2. What distracts and lures people away from God?

3. How do you deal with the setbacks
   and defeats in your life?

4. What person has greatly affected you to
   move closer or to grow in God?

5. In the Bible, is there a person that you relate to
   as a hero or example in following God? Why?

** **

"Do that which is

assigned you,

and you cannot

hope too much

or dare too much."

RALPH WALDO EMERSON,
AMERICAN POET AND PHILOSOPHER, 1803–1882

CHAPTER 4

R.I.P. MEANS "RETURNING IN POWER"

I HAVE NEVER HEARD an audible voice from God. However, the day after the drowning at the lake, I did sense an overwhelming "voice" speak to my spirit. I was at the peak of curiosity about what had happened to me when a voice said to me: "Had you not given your life to Me one month ago...yesterday would have been your reckoning day." Wow. Imagine hearing those words!

I had almost missed my opportunity to get right with God and make peace with heaven. It is important to understand: you can sin away your day of grace. At first, I did know there were actually verses in the Bible that explained this truth. In time, however, I found it throughout the Bible. God even warns, "My Spirit shall not strive with man forever, for he is indeed flesh" (Genesis 6:3a, NKJV).

The writer of Hebrews gives us a sober warning:

"If we deliberately keep on sinning after we have received the knowledge of the truth, no sacrifice for sins is left, but only a fearful expectation of judgment and of raging fire that will consume the enemies of God. Anyone who rejected the law of Moses died without mercy on the testimony of two or three witnesses. How much more severely do you think someone deserves to be punished who has trampled the Son of God underfoot, who has treated as an unholy thing the blood of the covenant that sanctified them, and who has insulted the Spirit of grace? For we know Him who said, 'It is mine to avenge; I will repay,' and again, 'The Lord will judge His people.' It is a dreadful thing to fall into the hands of the living God" (Hebrews 10:26-31).

This is not academic theory or dry theology. I almost sinned away my day of grace! But even as God is full of justice, He is also full of wonderful love! This is a truth I learned in the days and weeks that followed the day at the lake.

During my recovery time, I read my Bible and prayed more than ever before. One day while reading Revelation, the last book of the Bible, I recognized that the writer John had a similar experience to mine when he wrote about being "caught up" in heaven. I kept reading, and I saw another passage by John that captured my attention. John described a moment where he felt an overpowering love that staggered his understanding. It was exactly what I had felt that fateful day when I drowned in the lake. In his first letter to the churches, John wrote, "Perfect love expels all fear" (1 John 4:18, *NLT*). I suddenly realized that in my near-death encounter—as I had been looking at my body slowly being covered with dirt and sand and lying on the bottom of the lake—I had not been afraid. The love in the lake had fully enveloped me. There was no room for fear. Not long after I had fully recovered, I decided to enroll in Southwestern Bible College in Waxahachie, Texas. Eventually, I became a minister with the Assemblies of God. Through all the years that followed that near-death encounter at the lake to the present day, one realization has never left me: *I died and my life was given back*. I know there is life beyond the grave; I know there is much more to life than what we are experiencing right now. I do not fear dying, but await my "second journey" with great anticipation. I know what I saw. I shook hands with death and learned wonderful, life-changing lessons.

OUR APPOINTMENT

We all have an appointment with death. The writer of Hebrews noted, "And as it is appointed for men to die once, but after this the judgment" (Hebrews 9:27 *NKJV*). We all know what an appointment is—a scheduled meeting, often on a daily basis. We have an appointed time to be at work, to go home, to eat and to sleep. If I call the doctor's office and ask for an appointment, a time is chosen for me to go, and I keep that appointment—I usually get there early. My friend, Troy Korsgaden, taught me, "If you aren't five minutes early, you're late."

The word "appointed" in the Hebrews passage is an adjective meaning "chosen or agreed." It is talking about a different kind of appointment. I can call to cancel an appointment with the doctor, but this appointment, the one with God, cannot be cancelled. It is a done deal.

Comedian George Allen said: "I don't mind dying, I just don't want to be there when it happens." We all fear how we're going to die. Most people, I assume, just want to fall asleep and stop breathing...that is what my mom believed and wanted, and she got it. But actually, how we die is one thing that is out of our hands. Solomon said, "As no one has power over the wind to contain it; so no one has power over the time of their death" (Ecclesiastes 8:8). King Solomon even added, "It is better to go to a house of mourning than to go to a house of feasting, for death is the destiny of everyone; the living should take this to heart" (Ecclesiastes 7:2).

> *Comedian George Allen said: "I don't mind dying, I just don't want to be there when it happens."*

As a pastor of a large church in central California, I have the privilege of hearing every week about children being born. Even if a child was conceived in the worst of families, there is still a great celebration over the birth. But King Solomon said, "A good name is better than fine perfume, and the day of death better than the day of birth" (Ecclesiastes 7:1). In other words, our joy ought to be on a greater scale when we die. It is a homecoming where the Lord is waiting to greet us. We all have an appointment with death, but dying is not to be feared. Living is more than this life alone. God's love has no equal. God is in the business of bringing people back. I came back in His power. The passions that shape my life have been fueled by God giving me a second chance.

I CAME BACK TO BE A SOUL WINNER

Shortly after my near-death experience, I did not have a clue as to where to go or what to do. I knew that I needed to make money to survive. I enrolled in the local junior college thinking it would help me find a career later. One thing I did know: I didn't want to be poor. My dad was always broke and I decided that I was not going to be broke. I thought, *What is worse than being broke?* I didn't take into account that my dad had eight children. Having eight crumb-snatchers will make anyone go broke! About this time, I discovered a love for working with the youth at my church. I began training as a Royal Ranger commander. The Royal Rangers are a worldwide para-church ministry of the Assemblies of God devoted to sharing Christ with young people through the use of camping and the outdoors. For me, the experience proved invaluable in learning how to lead kids to Christ.

One of the worship leaders at my church had noticed me working with young boys on Wednesday night. He saw God's touch on my life, and encouraged me to seriously consider going to Bible college. It was God prompting him to share with me…a true "God nudge." As mentioned earlier, I decided to attend Bible college in Waxahachie, Texas, and at my new church home, I instantly became a Royal Ranger commander. Together with my team of commanders, we led hundreds of young boys into a relationship with Christ.

When I left the Royal Rangers, I became a youth pastor. I worked nine years in youth camps and in churches. During that time, I was able to pray with hundreds, leading them to faith in Jesus Christ. The first church where my wife Karen and I pastored involved five wonderful years in making disciples for Christ and encouraging God's people in their commitment to Him. I often think about the people that I led to Christ in those early years. I wonder how and when they would have found their way to God had I died on the bottom of muddy Lake O' the Pines? To God be all the glory!

One day, the Holy Spirit impressed upon me and Karen to leave our first pastorate and start a church in Oceanside, California. It was a big move. I knew that in order to plant a church, we would need a substantial amount of money. I pondered, *How am I ever going to raise enough money?* Then, I had an idea—a God-inspired idea. I would create a drama on the coming of Jesus to the earth and take it on the road. We travelled around for about six months performing that drama. We saw almost 1,000 people profess faith in Jesus Christ and we collected enough financial support to begin our new ministry. We started Family Fellowship Church in Oceanside and led thousands to faith in Jesus Christ. The church remains a lighthouse to the community and many folks trained in those days serve in full-time ministry today.

My near-death experience makes me want to tell everyone, "Get your reservations in for eternity and ask for the non-smoking section!"

As of this writing, Karen and I have been pastoring for five years in Visalia, California. We have multiple weekend services with thousands in attendance and not a service has slipped by that we have not had people accept Jesus Christ as Lord and Savior. It is not uncommon to see 100 people a weekend get right with God. Hardly a month goes by that we don't baptize at least 25 people in water because they have decided to follow Jesus.

If you ask me what was the most obvious change that occurred in my life after my near-death encounter at 19, I would have to say I became passionate about soul winning! My near-death experience and thousands of other people with a similar NDE history have come to understand that heaven is real and that one day we are either going to heaven or going to hell. My near-death experience makes me want to tell everyone, "Get your reservations in for eternity and ask for the non-smoking section!"

I CAME BACK TO HELP THE LESS FORTUNATE

Twenty years ago, I was a simple pastor in Texas minding my own business and serving God's Kingdom when God gave me a prompting to help my friend Ken Squires, who was starting a ministry called Sun City. We took teens and young adults to Mexico and other countries in order to expose them to short-term missions work.

Acting on God's nudge, I called Ken. He pleaded with me to come help him go into Mexico and meet with pastors in very poor places. I agreed. Over the next five years it was my job to set up sites where youth pastors could bring a group of Americans to spend a week with those who were in less fortunate situations. We planted five churches during those years. Today each church provides a much-needed ministry in the poor barrios of Mexico.

Coming back from my NDE has always made me sensitive to help the less fortunate. Even as Karen and I became the lead pastors at Visalia First Assembly in Visalia, California, we have supported hundreds of para-church organizations. Today over 100 organizations receive a monthly check from us—all of it from God's hand and generosity.

I CAME BACK TO PASS THE BATON

There was a time when I had grown tired of pastoring. After 15 years of pastoring in Oceanside, I found myself disillusioned with the younger generation. The "seeker sensitive" movement was taking over the church. People were very concerned about being sensitive to those who were pre-Christian. We set out coffee, shortened the length of our church service and we even changed our language to be more hip. One day, Karen and I looked at each other out of frustration with the church and decided that we were not cut out to be seeker sensitive. I would even say, "We can leave it to younger pastors who have a burden for that style of church, but it's just not us."

About this time an opportunity arose to become the Vice President of Advancement at Southwestern Assemblies of God University in Waxahachie, Texas. The timing seemed perfect. In my mind, I had checked out on being a pastor. *I must be getting too old for the next generation,* I thought. *It's time to move on; my work is done.*

Well, God certainly has a sense of humor. He immediately thrust us into a university environment. Suddenly we were surrounded by young adults with a totally different set of values. I was praying one day and the Lord began an inward dialogue with me about this generation. I felt like God was asking me a question: "Who else do you think is coming?" That was it...I got the message. In one sitting the Lord changed my mind and gave me a heart for the next generation. He was basically telling me: "No one else is coming. You have to pass the baton to them or you are going to end up dropping the baton between your generation and theirs."

From that day forward, I have crafted ways that I could get the next generation to take the baton. It is interesting...the older generation is looking back at the younger generation thinking they are not worthy enough to take the baton, while the younger generation is looking at the older generation saying: "Hurry up, old timer! Why are you so slow?"

If you visit our church in Visalia where we pastor today, you would see we are neither seeker sensitive nor seeker hostile. We like being a "Spirit sensitive" church. We believe that the Holy Spirit can work with those who are pre-Christian and He can do a much better job than a cup of coffee. Do not get me wrong, we still serve coffee today, but it is far from being the focus of our meeting. We are people who are hungry for more of God and less of this world.

One of the things Karen and I are on a mission to accomplish is to help the next generation understand the power of God's presence. We have spent our lives trying to help people comprehend God's presence in worship and daily living. We learned it in our generation and it is something we cannot afford to lose. Just look at Europe and the very small numbers of younger Christians, and you will have a perfect picture of one generation failing another when it comes to the presence of God. What a privilege to come back and serve Christ, and part of that privilege is to pass on the baton to the next generation.

I CAME BACK TO INSTILL
THE IMPORTANCE OF EDUCATION

When we became candidates to be the lead pastors of Visalia First Assembly, the church board asked us what our vision for the church was. I told them straight out that I did not have one. My vision at that time was wrapped up in the Bible college in Texas. However, I told them, "God has a vision for your church. He has had one for years. I would not feel right coming in and overlaying a vision on the church that was something that I had learned through the years. No, let's find out God's vision for Visalia First…together."

They elected us and we spent a few weeks praying and asking God what He wanted us to do. Quickly, we discovered that the education system was hurting in the Central Valley of California. Almost half of the people in our community did not complete high school. Upon further investigation, we also discovered that there was a profound disillusionment regarding public education. Hence, we began a journey on upgrading the education equivalency in our area. We began a charter school formulated on the basis of leadership and character. In our second year of operation, we turned away 200 students for lack of classroom space.

We also saw a need for improved Bible education in the region. We wanted believers to have a strong grounding in the Scriptures, understand the wonder of God's presence, be committed to prayer and fellowship, draw courage to evangelize, and show wisdom in distinguishing the temporal from the eternal. It resulted in establishing a new, accredited Bible college.

When I think about the Bible college, charter school, and desire to raise the level of education in the Central Valley, I know that I am alive today because God wanted me to be part of this good work. I am here to train the next generation.

I CAME BACK TO HELP PEOPLE
ESTABLISH MEMORIALS IN HEAVEN

I believe that one of my purposes in life is to get people to establish memorials in heaven. I read a book recently entitled *Revealing Heaven: An Eyewitness Account* (Xulon Press) by Kat Kerr. In that book the author talks about going to heaven and the memorials that have been established in heaven.

Bible students are familiar with the story of Cornelius in Acts, chapter 10. Cornelius was a God-fearing man who was known for giving back to his community. He was known to give generous amounts of his money to the neediest of people. Cornelius was also a good father and a great military leader. He was in charge of a battalion of Roman soldiers stationed at Caesarea. He was an important man, but inside he felt his life was empty. Even though Cornelius was a non-Jew, he had a hunger for more of God. One day while he was praying, an angel showed up and gave him some advice. (If you do not believe in angelic visits, you need to study up on it. It happens all the time.)

What the angel of the Lord said to Cornelius is interesting to note. After he got over his initial fear of seeing an angel, he asked what it was that the Lord wanted. Why the visit God? The Bible records that "Cornelius stared at him in fear. 'What is it Lord?' he asked. The angel answered, 'Your prayers and gifts to the poor have come up as a memorial offering before God'" (Acts 10:4).

Let me break it down for you: Cornelius attracted the attention of God because of his devotion and generosity. He was doing what most people who have had a near-death experience do when they come back: they become very generous. He, however, did not need a near-death experience to know how to make his life count for God. Jesus told Thomas, "'Because you have seen me, you have believed; blessed are those who have not seen and yet have believed'" (John 20:29).

But here is the best part—Cornelius had established some memorials in heaven. It is as if God was walking around in heaven one day and ran into the memorial that had been built in honor of all the work Cornelius had done for the poor. Can you hear God saying, "We've got do something for that boy." His memorial had become so big that Cornelius was attracting the attention of heaven. And the Gospel was opened up to the whole gentile world because of that act.

Just a point here: I do not know when it happened, but somewhere down the line in my life I became a very generous person. I have tried to trace it back as to when it started. I think it occurred when I had my near-death experience. Today, when I am being a giver, I have a strong, satisfying feeling deep inside of me...I feel close to God and feel like I am being like Him because God loves to give.

Stingy people really get under my skin. There is nothing more ungodly than being a greedy person. The most famous verse in the Bible is, "For God so loved the world that He gave His only begotten Son, that whoever believes in Him should not perish but have everlasting life" (John 3:16, *NKJV*). God was the first giver. He gave His son Jesus.

Seven years have elapsed since Karen and I left our work in Oceanside, but I was back there this summer. I visited the grave of a wealthy person I had known. I stayed there for an hour; I went there to find closure. We had struggled for years in church planting in Oceanside. This old fellow was a part of

He made it to heaven, I am sure of that, but he did not get there in great shape.

our church and had millions of dollars. I can't remember one offering that he gave to our church. When he died, all his money went to a distant relative and knowing that fact really got under my skin. We were doing the greatest work in the world (winning people to Jesus) and he showed no interest. How can you do that? How can you go all the way through life living in such a way that greed has taken such a strong hold on you, and that you do not want to help expand the work of God's Kingdom on the earth?

As I stood over his grave, I told him how much I struggled with his stinginess. I knew I could not leave until I got this out of my heart. And I did. I forgave the old farmer. I pledged that I would step it up when it came to talking to people about establishing memorials in heaven. He made it to heaven, I am sure of that, but he did not get there in great shape.

Jesus had a similar encounter with a rich young ruler in Matthew 19. On the surface, the young fellow was doing everything right to please God by following the commandments—but he was still missing the mark. When Jesus lovingly challenged him to give up the one item that was holding him back from following God, the young man went away sad. Jesus told him to sell his possessions and give to the poor in order to gain treasure in heaven, but he could not do it. He was holding on too tightly to things that are temporary, and he missed the eternal.

I have read and listened to hundreds who have had a near-death experience and visited the other side. I remember one lady describing memorials in heaven. She spoke about a person on the earth who had spent a great bit of time helping the less fortunate. She was able to visit that lady's memorial in heaven. "Quite impressive," she quipped.

Another memorial she described captured my attention. There was a huge fountain and some small pools were attached to the memorial. As you looked into the pools you did not see your own reflection but you saw the faces of all those who had been helped in some way by this individual. What the person had done on earth had been secured into a memorial in heaven. You could not only see the faces and expressions of the people that had been helped, but you could also hear words of gratitude as they spoke of the individual who helped them.

One of these days, you and I will be called to be with Jesus. I am not sure how things work in heaven, but I do know that I can affect the way I spend eternity. The old saying goes: "You can't take your money with you but you can send it on ahead." I encourage you with every fiber in my being, do something each day that helps the less fortunate. Do something that will advance the Kingdom of God on the earth. I give you the promise of Jesus that He gave to the rich young ruler: "Go, sell everything you have and give to the poor, and you will have treasure in heaven. Then come, follow me" (Mark 10:21).

RETURNING IN POWER

If you have ever been to an old cemetery you will note a good number of small tombstones with the initials R.I.P. etched into wood, granite, marble, bronze and iron. The letters stand for the words "Rest in Peace." Can you imagine if those letters stood for "Returning in Power?" I am a man who died and came back by God's grace and power. I was given a second chance to live for Him. I want to live passionately and powerfully for Christ. Everything I have shared with you so far reflects this change, but there are truths that you can take hold of...three powerful teachings that do not require a near-death experience. All you need is a willing heart.

PERSONAL QUEST

1. If you could do one great thing on behalf of God's grace toward you, what would you do out of gratitude for the Lord?

2. How does God measure success in a person's life?

3. Why is soul-winning such a powerful passion?

4. What other acts on earth build memorials in heaven?

5. Do you invest in another generation? If so, how?

***

"God loves you

just the way you are,

but he refuses to

leave you that way.

He wants you

to be just like Jesus."

MAX LUCADO,
CHRISTIAN INSPIRATIONAL WRITER, 1955

CHAPTER 5

GOD'S LOVE CHANGES EVERYTHING

"GUILT." SIMPLY SAYING THE WORD conjures up a lot of different feelings in people. You may have been raised where guilt was used to impress the importance of a matter or to get you to do something you did not really want to do. I was raised that way and lived with a guilty conscience all the time. I used to think: *If I ever run into God, the first thing He will want to talk to me about is my sins.* Even after I was born again, I had this nagging sense that I would never be able to pay off all the bad I had done in my life.

However, when I had my near-death experience at Lake O' the Pines, something amazing occurred—the watery lake lit up with God's light. Any thought of my sinful lifestyle was gone; sin was not part of the experience. I was enraptured by this newfound sense of God's love emanating from the light. I have come to understand this is a common occurrence of those who have had a near-death experience.

The Apostle John deeply understood the compelling power of God's love when he penned these words for us:

> "This is love: not that we loved God, but that He loved us and sent His Son as an atoning sacrifice for our sins. Dear friends, since God so loved us, we also ought to love one another. No one has ever seen God; but if we love one another, God lives in us and His love is made complete in us. This is how we know that we live in Him and He in us: He has given us of His Spirit. And we have seen and testify that the Father has sent His Son to be the Savior of the world. If anyone acknowledges that Jesus is the Son of God, God lives in them and they in God. And so we know and rely on the love God has for us. God is love. Whoever lives in love lives in God, and God in them. This is how love is made complete among us so that we will have confidence on the day of judgment: In this world we are like Jesus. There is no fear in love. But perfect love drives out fear, because fear has to do with punishment. The one who fears is not made perfect in love" (1 John 4:10-18).

Let me ask you a question: in your relationship with God who is more reliable and consistent in love? Is it you or God? It is a pretty easy question to answer. God is the more faithful lover. His love is always there for you even when you do not love Him. A lot of people will talk about God's faithful love on the surface, but sometimes I think that is happy-talk rather than bedrock conviction. It is not enough to just know that God loves us, we must believe it. Let me illustrate why this is so important.

JESUS ANNOUNCES A BETRAYER AT THE LAST SUPPER

Jesus walked the earth for three years with His disciples. Then, while He was having His last meal with His closest friends, He shocked the whole room by saying: "Before the night is over, one of you will betray Me." Even as they were still reeling from this unbelievable news, Jesus spoke about His impending demise by crucifixion. He basically said, "They are going to hang Me high and cut Me low boys, but there is one of you in this room who is going to betray Me before all that happens." Everyone began to look around the room, wondering who the

It is not enough to just know that God loves us, we must believe it. Let me illustrate why this is so important.

scoundrel might be. Peter and John—Jesus' closest friends—were shocked, but I think John was far more sure of himself than Peter with this news.

At the meal, John was leaning on Jesus' bosom. John was the youngest of the disciples and enjoyed hanging out with the

Lord. John had a close connection with Jesus and would not betray the Christ. How could John be confident enough to lean his head on Jesus' shoulder? What gave him such assurance? The secret of John's relationship with Jesus was simple: *John knew Jesus loved him.* Grasping this reality of God's deep unfailing love for you all the time, regardless of how you fare, brings GOOD things into your life—blessings that range from inner peace to boldness in sharing about the Lord.

The phrase about John as the disciple whom Jesus loved appears four times in the Gospel of John.

1. "One of them, the disciple whom Jesus loved, was reclining next to him" (John 13:23).

2. "When Jesus saw his mother there, and the disciple whom he loved standing nearby, he said to her, 'Woman, here is your son'" (John 19:26).

3. "Then the disciple whom Jesus loved said to Peter, 'It is the Lord!' As soon as Simon Peter heard him say, 'It is the Lord,' he wrapped his outer garment around him (for he had taken it off) and jumped into the water" (John 21:7).

4. "Peter turned and saw that the disciple whom Jesus loved was following them. (This was the one who had leaned back against Jesus at the supper and had said, 'Lord, who is going to betray you?')" (John 21:20).

It has always amused me that the one who repeatedly said, "The disciple whom Jesus loved," was the disciple whom Jesus loved.

That statement does not appear in the other Gospel accounts. John felt God's love. John knew Jesus' love for him was greater than his own love for God. John knew how deeply loved he was by Jesus, and that love changed everything.

Let me give you an example: let us say two of my pastor friends go to lunch with me. We have a great time of fellowship because we all follow Christ. I go home and write in my journal that night: *There were three of us, all pastors, who went to lunch today: Pastor Tom, Pastor Mark and...of course...the pastor whom Jesus really loves.* Well, that is what John did—he wrote down the undeniable truth—God simply, wonderful, richly loved John because "God is love."

Peter on the other hand had a different kind of relationship with Jesus. Peter had boasted days before that he would follow Jesus anywhere...that he would be faithful (see John 13:34-36). It was as if Peter had to prove his commitment to Jesus while everyone else could see John's commitment and love without John ever having to say a word.

Peter was a different story at this point in his relationship with Jesus; Peter felt emotionally distant. When you are insecure about being loved, you tend to overcompensate in conversation and feel guilty when there is not anyone actually accusing you. Peter did not have the courage to ask Jesus who the betrayer might be, so he motioned to John, "Ask Him which one He means" (John 13:24b). Jesus loved all the disciples intensely but where the other disciples failed to see the depth of that love, John was acutely aware of it—that gave John confidence in talking and being with Jesus.

Now consider how Peter boasted of his love for God and yet failed miserably that night when Jesus needed him the most (see Luke 22:60). When you boast of your love for God, such arrogance can lead you down a wrong path. On the other hand, when you boast of God's love for you and for others—you will be used in a great and mighty way. There is a confidence that comes when you tell others about the love that God has for them.

The great philosopher, Karl Barth, was asked to summarize the Christian life in one line. His answer was simple yet profound: "Jesus loves me this I know." Wow! What a statement.

BOAST OF HIS LOVE FOR YOU

Let us take this a step further. When Jesus began His ministry, He felt it imperative that He be baptized in water. Jesus went to visit his cousin, John, who was baptizing followers at the Jordan River, and requested to be baptized. When Jesus came out of the water of the Jordan River after being baptized, a voice from heaven (His Father) spoke over Jesus and said, "This is My Beloved Son, in whom I am well pleased" (Matthew 3:17b, KJV, NASB, NKJV).

Jesus heard His Father's approval. We all need to believe those words God spoke over Jesus. It surely was not because of the number of things Jesus did while He was on the earth, for He was barely getting His ministry started. Instead, Jesus knew He was loved by the Father, and the Father made it clear before others that He loved His only begotten Son. How we need to embrace that love from God. Even Paul understood this rich love when he wrote, "For it is by grace you have been saved, through faith—and this is not from yourselves, it is the gift of God—not by works, so that no one can boast" (Ephesians 2:8-9). God is the architect of salvation; we aren't. God offers salvation as a gift because He loves us, not because we love Him.

This is one point that we really need to grasp—we are not saved by works of righteousness (singing in the choir, helping the poor, being an usher at church) and other good deeds; it is only according to God's mercy we have been saved. You will never gain God's approval by works! We all have to come to the revelation that God loves us regardless of what we do for Him.

How many young people could win in life if they heard those words from the Father? "This is my son...this is my daughter...I am so pleased with him/her." It is hard being a teen and trying to figure life out. Teens seem to be in such a wilderness these days. But if they knew how much God loved them, they could handle temptation without breaking a sweat.

As soon as Jesus heard those words: "This is My beloved Son, with whom I am well pleased," He was led into the wilderness by the Holy Spirit. While He was there, an amazing thing began to occur...the devil showed up.

Teens seem to be in such a wilderness these days. But if they knew how much God loved them, they could handle temptation without breaking a sweat.

That's not the amazing thing because the devil shows up daily in my life too, but take note of what the Devil said to Jesus: "If you are the Son of God, command this stone to become bread" (Luke 4:3 *NKJV*).

Jesus combatted the devil's temptation with a few words He had learned Himself. "It is written, 'Man shall not live by bread alone, but by every word of God'" (v.4).

Satan then took Jesus up on a high mountain and showed Him all the kingdoms of the world in just a moment of time. Satan then said to Jesus: "All this authority I will give You, and their glory; for this has been delivered to me, and I give it to whomever I wish. Therefore, if You will worship before me, all will be Yours" (vv. 5-7).

Jesus' reply is classic: "Get behind Me, Satan! For it is written, 'You shall worship the Lord your God, and Him only you shall serve'" (v. 8).

You can feel the power in those words!

The third time Satan appeared to Jesus, he tried to get Jesus to commit suicide. "The devil led Him to Jerusalem and had Him stand on the highest point of the temple. "'If you are the Son of God throw Yourself down from here.' For it is written: 'He shall give His angels over You, to keep You,' and 'In their hands they shall bear You up, lest you dash Your foot against a stone'" (vv. 9-11).

Don't think for a minute that Satan does not know what the Bible says—he does. The key is to also know the Scripture so that you will be ready with a reply when you are tempted. Take a look at how Jesus answered Satan by quoting Scripture back at him: "It has been said, 'You shall not tempt the LORD your God'" (v. 12).

Jesus was not even tempted to kill Himself that day—He was not going to fall for the trickery of Satan. And do you know why He did not fall? It was because He had heard the voice from heaven just a few days earlier: "This is My beloved Son in whom I am well pleased." The tempter cannot be successful when you know you are loved of God. You have to walk through this life believing that you are loved of God.

Let us say you go to have coffee with a few of your closest friends, and you are having the time of your life. Three hours go by and you do not even realize that much time has passed. You do not want to go home because you are having fun. Why do you think that is? Think about it: while you may not have realized it, you were having fun and time seemed to stand still because you were sitting with friends who did not judge you. We all do better when we live in a way that serves the God of love and not a God of judgment.

Years ago I read this advertisement that appeared in a newspaper of a major city in Mexico:

PACO, I LOVE YOU. ALL IS FORGIVEN. PLEASE COME HOME. IF YOU READ THIS ADVERTISEMENT, MEET ME AT THE TOWN SQUARE...

It also listed the date and time. It was signed, "Your father." Apparently, a young man had run away from home. In an attempt to see him again, his father placed this ad with the hope of reaching his son. Guess what happened on the day that Paco was supposed to meet his dad? More than 30 young men by the name of Paco showed up in the town square! I am convinced that if we knew how much God loves us we would do a whole lot better in life. You may not have that revelation yet, but God will give it to you if you ask Him.

If you are a student of the Bible you will remember what happened after Jesus was betrayed, crucified and resurrected. Who was the first person Jesus wanted to see on His 50-day tour of the Holy Land? It was the man who had betrayed Him just before He died—Peter.

Take a look at the conversation that Jesus had with Peter:

"'When they had finished eating, Jesus said to Simon Peter, 'Simon son of John, do you love me more than these?' 'Yes, Lord,' he said, 'You know that I love you.' Jesus said, 'Feed my lambs.' Again Jesus said, 'Simon son of John, do you love me?' He answered, 'Yes, Lord, you know that I love you.' Jesus said, 'Take care of my sheep.' The third time he said to him, 'Simon son of John, do you love me?' Peter was hurt because Jesus asked him the third time, 'Do you love me?' He said, 'Lord, You know all things; You know that I love you.' Jesus said, 'Feed my sheep'" (John 21:15-17).

You would not see this in a casual reading of the text, but Jesus is interchanging the Greek words for love. He begins by asking Peter if he *agape* Him. There are four major words used in the Greek to describe love and the one used here is agape, the highest form of love there is—an unconditional love. That is the kind of love that God has for each of us—unconditional, unwavering, and unbreakable.

Peter answered Jesus with a different Greek word for love: *phileo*, a brotherly type of love. This is the root word for the word "Philadelphia," which means city of brotherly love.

Jesus asked a second time: "Peter, do you agape Me?" Peter replied, "Yes, Lord I phileo You." At that point, Jesus knew that Peter had an on-board computer glitch so He changed His word for love when He asked Peter a third time. "Peter, do you phileo Me?" Amazing! Jesus knew that Peter still did not have the revelation about love that John had come to grasp—John knew he was loved by God. In contrast, Peter was still struggling, especially since he had just denied Jesus a week earlier.

Jesus changed the word because He was willing to come down to Pete's level to bring him up to the agape level. That is the way God is—He reaches out to us where we are at in life and He lifts us up simply because He loves us. Maybe you were raised in a guilt-ridden environment…maybe you have struggled with God's love because you struggled with your relationship with your earthly father…but God's rich and unfailing love is there for you.

I encourage you to pause before you continue and ask God to help you understand how much He loves you. Good things happen to those who know they are loved by God. "And now these three remain: faith, hope and love. But the greatest of these is love" (1 Corinthians 13:13).

HIS LOVE MAKES US AUDIBLE READY

Let me ask you a question: Do you know what 'Audible Ready' means? When football quarterbacks come up to the line to run a play, they eye the defense. If the quarterback sees something he does not like in the defense he can call an audible. It simply means he will change the play while at the line. The only catch is that the team has to be audible ready.

When I came to understand the faithful love of God I found myself wanting to serve Him more, and I knew that to serve Him was to listen closely to His signals—His will. God's love has that effect…we want to know and please Him more and serve those around us. In the Bible, Luke writes about one of Israel's greatest heroes who understood the importance of listening to God's will—he was audible ready. Luke says about David that after "he had served his own generation by the will of God, he fell asleep" (Acts 13:36, *NKJV*). These fourteen words, this one sentence, has become one of my life verses. This passage of Scripture is loaded with content; you can miss it with a casual glance. The Bible says David "served." Why is it that the writer of the Book of Acts, inspired by the Holy Spirit, chose to represent David in this manner? David did a lot of great things in his lifetime. Why didn't Luke say: "David, the one who slew Goliath when the army of Israel was frozen with fear and afraid to act." I think that's a pretty good way to remember David.

When I came to understand the faithful love of God I found myself wanting to serve Him more, and I knew that to serve Him was to listen closely to His signals—His will.

Why didn't Luke talk about the largest offering ever given to a church in the Bible? I think it still stands as the largest offering on record today. David, at the end of his life, took all he had amassed and gave it to his son Solomon to build a massive temple where people could meet with God. Luke did not mention the offering or the Temple.

Why didn't he talk about David's military abilities? David was one bad motor scooter. When he and God hooked up there was not a more feared general of an army on the earth at that time. God made David the most successful Israelite warrior in history. But the writer did not mention that ability.

Why didn't he talk about David's songwriting skills? He wrote many of the psalms in the Bible. David could play a harp, and his playing skill was so exceptional that he was called to the king's palace. In Saul's home, David would play music to ward off the evil spirit that accompanied King Saul. The list of David's accomplishments goes on and on, but that is not what David is remembered for in the Bible. Instead, Dr. Luke calls David "a servant."

Knowing God's love is life-changing and the hallmark begins with serving others in His name. Touched by God's love in his teenage years as a shepherd, David was deeply moved to serve and to be sensitive to God's will. Of course, Jesus was the greatest servant of all. He says in Mark 9:35: "Anyone who wants to be first must be the very last, and the servant of all." In other words, the way up in the Kingdom is down. In Philippians, chapter 2, the Apostle Paul exhorts Christians to have the same attitude as Jesus—an attitude to serve wholeheartedly. My prayer is that God's immeasurable love will touch your heart...that you will hear the Good News and be audible ready as His servant on the field of life.

WE LOVE HIM BECAUSE HE LOVED US FIRST

David served "by the will of God" and that wasn't always understood by those around him. When David was beginning his reign as King of Israel, he was very intent on bringing the Ark of the Covenant to Jerusalem. It was common knowledge that wherever the Ark of the Covenant was located was where God's presence dwelt. After a failed first attempt to bring the Ark into Jerusalem, David tried again. This time he did it according to the rules established by Moses, and God was pleased by it. David was exhilarated over the Ark of the Covenant entering the new capital of the nation.

As David approached the city with the Ark in the procession, he did something very uncharacteristic for a king: he took off his outer garment, stripped down to his underwear, and danced before the Lord with all his might. His joy for the Lord was evident to all—he was in love with the God who first loved him. However, his first wife Michal looked out the window and despised him in her heart. Michal did not have a heart to seek after the presence of God; instead, she criticized her husband.

You could hear a pin drop when David got home for dinner that night as Michal let David have it: "How the King of Israel has distinguished himself today, going around half-naked in full view of the slave girls of his servants as any vulgar fellow would!" (2 Samuel 6:20).

David gave a quick response: "'It was before the Lord, who chose me rather than your father or anyone from his house when he appointed me ruler over the Lord's people Israel—I will celebrate before the Lord. I will become even more undignified than this and I will be humiliated in my own eyes. But by these slave girls you spoke of, I will be held in honor" (vv. 21-22).

You see, David did not serve after the will of his wife that day. Instead, David served after God's will. In his service to God, David had many opportunities to fulfill the requests made of him by friends and family, but David always tried to serve God's will first. David was audible ready. Believe me, when God's love works through you, your priorities are made straight and blessings always follow.

GOD'S LOVE OPENS OUR EYES

A lot of people do not understand God. To illustrate, I want you to do something…take your thumb and index finger and put them into a position where an inch of space is between them. Now, take a look at the space between them and let's call it: "what I know about God." Now take a look at all the space that exists outside your index finger and thumb and think of that ongoing space as everything you do not know about God. The contrast is overwhelming—we simply understand a tiny fraction of God's mind, power and unfailing love. The prophet Isaiah moved by God's Spirit says it best: "'For my thoughts are not your thoughts, neither are your ways my ways,' declares the LORD. 'As the heavens are higher than the earth, so are my ways higher than your ways and my thoughts than your thoughts'" (Isaiah 55:8-9).

I have spent much of my life trying to tap into the incredible power of God that resides just outside of our understanding. You and I have five senses—we can taste, touch, smell, hear and see. We perceive our world through these five senses. Now the sixth sense has always interested me—the supernatural awareness of a dynamic, spiritual world connected to our physical one. But if I don't understand it all...that's okay. What I do need to grasp most of all is how much I am loved by God.

When I was growing up, certain things were placed into my psyche. I grew up dealing with a lot of guilt and condemnation. I viewed God as more of an ogre rather than the God of love and grace. Yet my life took a different path, and those early perceptions of God changed. I still haven't grasped the full depth, height or width of the love that God has for me and for each one of us, but I know that God's great love transforms the hardest heart and most stubborn mind. I remember something that Dr. Mike Smalley said at Southwestern Assemblies of God University (SAGU) in Waxahachie, Texas. During the chapel service he made a powerful statement. I think it is revolutionizing: "Nothing you can do changes God's love for you!"

No matter who you are or what you have done, God is radically in love with you and you can't change that! You can walk outside right now and smoke a joint of marijuana and God will still love you. You can go on a drunken binge for three weeks and God still loves you. You can spend two hours in church praying and speaking in tongues and God still loves you the same as He did when you were not in church. You may be considered one of the greatest people on earth. You may be an accomplished leader, have a fantastic resumé the length of your arm, or succeed in curing a disease like cancer...it does not matter more or less, because God loves you because He is love.

Success in life is not guaranteed just because God loves you. God loving you has little to do with you succeeding or failing in life. You can go your whole life doing everything wrong and God will still love you. You can go your whole life doing everything right and God will still love you. God loves you because He is love, and He never falters in giving His love.

Years ago my body sank in a lake so that God could sink into my heart the depth of His unfailing love. When His love begins to sink into your heart…when you come to grasp how deep the love of God is for you…everything will change. You will find strength to go on the heights; you will be as nimble as a deer and as bold as a lion. You will find an inner peace that surpasses understanding, because you are not alone. God's love transforms us and by His good will we serve the generation in which we are born.

PERSONAL QUEST

1. Does God draw men to Him with love first or with judgment? Why? How?

2. In 1 Corinthians, chapter 13, it says that God's "love never fails" and this passage is a favorite for many people. What does that mean for you?

3. Where do you experience God's love on a daily basis?

4. How would or does a relationship with God and His love affect your perception of your parents and people in your life?

5. How do you express your love of God at home, work and church?

***

"There comes a time in life

when we are tapped

on the shoulder for a moment

that is unique to us.

Woe to those who are

unprepared for what could

have been their finest hour."

WINSTON CHURCHILL,
BRITISH PRIME MINISTER, 1874–1965

CHAPTER 6

THE MAD DASH BETWEEN THE DATES

I HAVE ALWAYS BEEN CURIOUS about cemetery headstones. I think that what is etched, carved or fashioned into the headstone about a person's life is a kind of old fashioned Twitter tweet...a short line or two to sum up one's life. Being in a cemetery and seeing the names of people who have come before us always raises questions. We become introspective and ponder our existence with thoughts like, *Why am I taking up space on the planet? Is there a real purpose to my life?* or *What will be on my headstone when I die?*

Years ago I was attending a funeral with my nieces and nephews, and we had gone out to the cemetery to say our last good-byes to a relative. After the service, I walked around the cemetery looking at the headstones. I found a headstone in the

far back corner of the cemetery that really did not say much,
but something captured my imagination about this particular
stone. The headstone had the date of the person's birth and then
it had the date of the person's death. However, the line between
the dates was out of character. Most tombstones do not have a
hyphen between the dates, or if they do, it is usually just a little
short hyphen. But not this headstone, it had a line between the
dates that must have been 18 inches long!

You are responsible for what occurs between your birth and death in this world. What are you doing with the mad dash?

That's when it occurred to me…you cannot
choose the date you are born, and you cannot choose the date that you die. The only
thing you get to choose…the only thing
you do have power over is "the mad dash
between the dates!" You are responsible for
what occurs between your birth and death
in this world. What are you doing with the
mad dash? Are you working to apply all your talents and abilities
to make your life count for something?

Ever wonder why some people have nothing written upon
their tombstone? Either they did not plan to have anything written or there was not anything of merit to place on it. There is
a quote that is partially attributed to the late American writer
Henry David Thoreau and to the late Supreme Court Justice
Oliver Wendell Holmes that simply states: "Most people lead

lives of quiet desperation, and go to their graves with the song still in their heart." What a tragedy! Imagine not fulfilling your purpose in life!

Someone once said that the Dead Sea with all its minerals and sediments is quite possibly the wealthiest place on the planet. I would have to disagree. I believe local graveyards in every town hold the greatest wealth on the planet. Buried deep below the ground are a lot of people who went to their graves with their life's music still locked away within them! How sad. Buried is the greatest song that was never sung...the greatest book that was never penned...the greatest speech that was never spoken. All that wealth of the human spirit is buried and forever silent.

It is imperative that we discover why we are on this planet. We are not here to simply take up space. We have a purpose. While working as a vice president of Southwestern Assemblies of God University (SAGU) in Waxahachie, Texas, I often ran into young people who were trying to figure out their life's purpose. Our SAGU President, Dr. Kermit Bridges, often offered this exhortation: "You are in the decade of decision. What you do between the ages 16-26 determines what you do for the rest of your life."

There are three decisions that impact your effectiveness on earth. If you can discover the answer to these three things you will be ahead of most people. Here is what you have to decide:

- Will you serve God or not?

- Who will you marry (if you are
  supposed to get married)?

- What career path will you choose?

If you do not remember anything else I say in this book, remember this, as it is too important to miss: *God has specific things that each of us have been assigned to do. Everything God created has an assignment. What is your assignment?*

THE UNCHANGING FACTS IN YOUR ASSIGNMENT

The number one question I get asked as a pastor is "What is God's will for my life?" While some give great attention to this question there are others seemingly who are not concerned. There are some people who find job ads in the newspaper to be the only source of purpose and direction. That is a very sad situation. I hope I can spur you on to discover your "Assignment"—God's unique design and call on your life here on earth—because that is where you will find great peace and gratification.

First, your Assignment is not your decision; it is your discovery. God has a plan for your life but you have to discover it. This is not the same as salvation. Salvation is God's intention, but our decision. It is God's intention that you be born again but it remains your decision to cooperate with Him and accept Jesus in your heart.

It is important to grasp this truth: your Assignment was decided before birth! Your Manufacturer designed you for a purpose. You are not *the* manufacturer, you are the product of a loving Manufacturer. He conceptualized you, designed your specifications, and built you to run a certain way. Think about it this way: did the automobile instruct Henry Ford as to what it should be? Did the airplane inform the Wright brothers as to what it would be?

Think about it this way: did the automobile instruct Henry Ford as to what it should be? Did the airplane inform the Wright brothers as to what it would be?

Furthermore, anything created or made cannot be used without instruction…without someone providing the blueprint as to how the product works, its warnings, and wisdom in keeping the product in tip-top operation. What if for the first time in your life you discovered a word processing computer. Your first reaction would be to stare at it. You would not know what it is, what to call it, and even have a clue as to how to turn it on. The buttons on the keyboard would be a foreign language to you. What is 'ALT?' What is 'DEL?' What is 'ESC?' There would be only two ways to figure out what that computer is and does. You could read the instruction manual or you could ask someone who is trained in computers to tell you what a computer is about and how to operate it.

The same goes for us as individuals. Let us go to the Manufacturer's guide—*The Holy Bible*—and begin to discover what our Designer designed us to do. Your Assignment has already been decided. Before grandpa Willie winked at your grandma Nelly, God had a plan for your life. One of my favorite passages in the Bible is found in Jeremiah:

> "The word of the LORD came to me, saying, 'Before I formed you in the womb I knew you, before you were born I set you apart; I appointed you as a prophet to the nations.' 'Alas, Sovereign LORD,' I said, 'I do not know how to speak; I am too young.' But the LORD said to me, 'Do not say, 'I am too young.' You must go to everyone I send you to and say whatever I command you. Do not be afraid of them, for I am with you and will rescue you,' declares the LORD. Then the LORD reached out his hand and touched my mouth and said to me, 'I have put my words in your mouth. See, today I appoint you over nations and kingdoms to uproot and tear down, to destroy and overthrow, to build and to plant.'" (Jeremiah 1:4-10).

YOUR ASSIGNMENT IS TO BE A PROBLEM-SOLVER

Problems always require problem-solvers. Mechanics solve automobile problems, attorneys solve legal problems, and accountants solve tax problems. Products we make solve problems: combs are used to untangle hair, spatulas are used to easily flip food over in a frying pan, and wallets and purses are used to hold money and credit cards. Even the parts of our body address problems: our eyes measure distance and enable us to drive cars, our noses identify rotting objects and enable us to eat healthily, and our feet and legs enable us to live in tall buildings because we can go up and down stairwells. Life is full of problems, and solutions are needed. When it comes to God…everything He designs meets a problem, a need, or a role. Here is the question you must ask yourself: What problem has your life been created to solve?

Many people have "go-yonder" eyes. If I could just go yonder to that city or that country then I could make something of myself. This is not true. I believe you have to blossom where you are, regardless of how you got there. Your Assignment is geographical. God made places before He made people. "From one man He made all the nations, that they should

Here is the question you must ask yourself: What problem has your life been created to solve?

inhabit the whole earth; and He marked out their appointed times in history and the boundaries of their lands. God did this so that they would seek Him and perhaps reach out for Him and find Him, though He is not far from any one of us, 'For in him we live and move and have our being'" (Acts 17:26-28). You may be exactly where God wants you to be and not know it!

Years ago I used to sit back and wonder what it would have been like to live in a different time period. I wondered what it would have been like in the year 1700 or even in a future year like 2100. I think I could have enjoyed living in the time of Christ. To be able to attend one of the Jesus Evangelist Crusades would have been incredible! To watch Him cast out demons, heal sick people, and fill people with wisdom from the ages...what an experience that would have been! Then it dawned on me that I am living exactly where and when I am supposed to be living. God did not choose to place me in the time of Christ in the middle of Judea, or in the time of King Louis XIV of France. He placed me in this time period to serve this generation.

Now think about the Bible story about Isaac's son Jacob. He was a young man on a road trip en route to see relatives. He has an encounter with God and the Bible records the following: "When Jacob awoke from his sleep, he thought, 'Surely the LORD is in this place, and I was not aware of it.' He was afraid and said, 'How awesome is this place! This is none other than the house of God; this is the gate of heaven'" (Genesis 28:16-17). You may be in the right place but feel afraid...that is okay because God is there with you.

You may also say: "I don't like where I am and who I am working for." My mom had a saying: "You can get happy in the same britches that you got mad in." This taught me a great lesson: We all must "get happy" where we are planted, because where you are is where you are. Maybe God has you in a place of servanthood at the moment. For example, God placed me in a position to serve a fellow minister for five years. Many times I wanted to leave that position but God was using him to make me a better person. Then the day came when I was released from serving that pastor and became a senior pastor myself. Someone said to me: "You will not be promoted until you become overly qualified in your present position." This gave me the fuel I needed to be happy and content in my current position.

CLUES TO YOUR ASSIGNMENT

There are many clues in discerning God's Assignment for you.

First, what you love and have a passion to embrace, be around, serve and watch over is a clue to your Assignment from God. It is never about money when you truly love someone or love doing something. If you have a love for children you will find yourself with them. If you have a passion for animals you will work in a kennel. If you love yard work you will be a landscaper. If heart surgery fascinates you, you will study to be a surgeon.

Second, the reverse of what you love is true—what you hate can be a clue to something you are assigned to correct. There are numerous examples that highlight this principle. Nehemiah could not sleep at night over the broken walls of Jerusalem and later would be the one to rebuild those walls. Abraham Lincoln hated seeing slavery as a young man and would later free all slaves in the U.S. when he became the nation's 16th president. Candy Lightner, a mother of three children, was determined to make a difference against drunk driving after her 13-year-old daughter, Cari, had been killed while walking in a residential California neighborhood—Candy started MADD (Mothers Against Drunk Driving). Many people stay in certain positions that may be disgusting, heartwrenching, and disturbing. If they took time to think it out carefully, however, they may discover that they are in that very position because God called them to solve a terrible problem.

The third clue is where you are celebrated—where you are affirmed for some quality or service that is true to your nature and work history. Being celebrated does not happen right away, you may have to endure being tolerated by those who do not want you to speak the truth, to do your work with excellence, or to show genuine care for coworkers. In those environments, you may walk into a room and feel the stares of everyone on you. You may enter a circle of friends and feel more like the proverbial 'fifth wheel' who is out of place. These are instances when you can sense you are being tolerated and not celebrated. You may be in a rough situation right now, but I promise that if you keep your heart right with God, someone, someday, somewhere will celebrate you. If you can begin to see yourself as a reward to someone, you will see a day where you are celebrated. That celebration will come quicker than you think—simply be faithful, thankful, serving as to the Lord.

RIGHT ENVIRONMENT IS AN ASSIGNMENT NECESSITY

Do you know the state bird of Florida? I humorously think it is the mosquito. Where I live in Central California, the mosquito cannot survive because we do not have an environment where it can thrive. In Florida, however, the weather can be hot, humid, and swampy—it's mosquito heaven. It needs swamp water and plenty of blood—preferably unsuspecting tourists. You can kill a single mosquito, but if you do not kill its breeding environment then thousands of mosquitos will follow.

When it comes to knowing your Assignment from God, finding the right climate is important. One of the most important things you can do for your Assignment is to get around those who have a similar calling. If you want to be an accountant, get around accountants. If you want to be a chef, go to culinary school. If you want to be a preacher, go to Bible School. Until you get in a climate where your calling is celebrated you use up valuable time in self-discovery. Someone said: "Experience is the best teacher."

I like to think that the experience of others is the best teacher. Many have gone to the school of hard knocks and have endured enormous amounts of pain to get where they are today. I don't like pain. However, I like it when I can learn from the pain of others rather than unnecessarily repeating those painful experiences on my own.

Your Assignment involves an environment where you can grow. And the good news is that both weakness and strength are nurtured in this environment. Jeremiah said, "'Alas, Sovereign Lord,' I said, 'I don't know how to speak, I am too young'" (Jeremiah 1:6). We are all intimidated about doing things that are "out of our league" in life. This was surely the case in Jeremiah's call. He ministered to a number of Jewish kings who were not receptive to his message. Yet, Jeremiah's weakness was strengthened by God's presence. When you are in the right environment the best comes out of you regardless of obstacles. When you are in the wrong environment the worst comes out of you regardless of perks. One of the greatest reasons I keep showing up at church is because that is an environment that is fostering the call of God on my life.

GOOD LISTENING IS AN ASSIGNMENT NECESSITY

Your Assignment also calls for you to listen to those around you. I love the Bible and have read it numerous times. All the Bible characters speak deeply to me. I have not met them face to face, but each one has mentored me from a distance. If I listen to them, I am all the better for it. In the Bible, Naaman was a great general with a lot of pride. The prophet of God told him that if he wanted to be healed he needed to take seven dips in a muddy pond. He was not going to do it but he listened to a servant girl and in doing so...he was healed.

We have to develop our listening skills because it enriches our capacity to fulfill the Assignment God gives us. Here is a tip to all of you who are married: listen to your mate. I was not half the man I am today until I got married. My wife is the best thing that has ever happened to my development in becoming the man that God wants me to be. I have not always agreed with her, but God has used her countless times to develop me in a manner that has prepared me for my current assignment. That is why you do not marry someone you are too comfortable with. You do not need to marry a "yes" person; you need to marry someone who is strong enough to correct you.

One of the greatest tragedies in life occurs when students do not listen to their parents. We have all grown up thinking that our parents were not cool and surely not up to date. I have some advice for you: your parents are not as dumb as you think they are. You may say, "My parents make my life miserable. I can't stand them." Have you ever stopped and pondered that statement? Your parents love you. Why would they have given birth to you and then make it their life-long pursuit to make your life miserable? Maybe God gave you those parents because they are exactly what is needed to develop you for your Assignment from God. Your ability to succeed is dependent upon an environment where you are challenged and upon your ability to accept correction.

GOOD PAIN IS AN ASSIGNMENT NECESSITY

Your Assignment will call you into some painful preparation. Former NFL Coach Tom Landry made this statement: "Champions do what they hate...to create what they love." He explained, "This is my job: I take players who want to win the Superbowl, and I make them do what they hate in order to become Superbowl champions." Champions are not created in the ring, but in the daily routine. That is why you never see joggers smiling, because they are in the routine of discipline. Do not ever think that preparation time is wasted time. I think you can never get prepared enough. Winners are some of the most over prepared people on the planet.

My friend Sam Chand says: "You will only grow to the level of your threshold of pain." When the pain gets to a place where you can no longer bear it, you have reached your stepping off place. In order to do great things you have to become a manager of pain. Get used to pain. You can pay now and play later.

Another point to consider: if you rebel against your Assignment, God may permit a painful experience to correct you. This is a different painful experience. When we do not discipline ourselves to endure the pain of gain then we take a different journey of pain and it may cost us a lot more. The psalmist said: "Before I was afflicted I went astray, but now I obey your word. It was good for me to be afflicted so that I might learn your decrees" (Psalm 119:67,71).

TIME IS AN ASSIGNMENT NECESSITY

Your Assignment will take time to fulfill—you need to be patient, persistent, and wise in the use of that time. Mexico has the peso. America has the dollar. Europe has the euro. Our earthly existence has a currency, too: The currency of this earthly reality is time. God did not give you friends, but He gave you the time to make friends. God did not give you money, but He gave you time to make money. You have to take time to develop your Assignment or it is not going to happen. Your Assignment may require more time than you realize…preparation time…negotiation time. Just as there are four seasons in a year there are multiple seasons is your Assignment. There are seasons of insignificance; seasons of meditation and seasons of agitation.

CLARITY IS AN ASSIGNMENT NECESSITY

Last, if you are going to get into your Assignment, you have to unclutter your day so you can clearly see, hear and know God's will in your life. Eliminate anything that does not involve God. Guard access to your life: Not everyone in your life is there to aid in your God-given assignment. Those who gain access must desire what you possess or must possess something you desire.

Here is a good exercise: Focus on creating a perfect day by planning your next 24 hours. Start your first hour of movement toward God—what you can do in the morning time. This is where you refocus your priorities in Christ, and share your concerns with God. One hour of movement toward health—do this at lunch today. You do not have to eat everything on your plate but take note of what you eat. Take one hour of movement toward a mentor—listen to a CD or a podcast and be open to learn and challenged to grow. Carve out one hour of movement toward a loved one—take your spouse on a date. This is where you reaffirm and remind one another of what God has given you in having the other as a mate. One hour of movement toward financial security—find a financial mentor where you can gain wisdom in how to use and grow your resources. One hour of movement toward relaxation—schedule a walk in a park and simply enjoy the beauty God puts before you.

ESTABLISH A LIFE MISSION STATEMENT

There is a practice that may refine and help focus your Assignment from God...it is in the creation of a mission statement. We can learn about mission statements from the most successful companies and organizations today.

Mission statements are powerful declarations. It is most often written with a line or two or a short paragraph with an occasional motto. The mission statement serves to remind founders and those who follow to pursue the highest excellence in building a product or in providing a service. The mission statement is the core, the identity and values of an organization. The Campbell Soup Company has a compelling line: "Nourishing people's lives everywhere, every day."[1] Starbucks, the coffee giant that seems to be on every corner, has a mission statement that says, "Our mission is to inspire and nurture the human spirit—one person, one cup, and one neighborhood at a time."[2] America's beloved Harley-Davidson Motorcycles says, "We ride with our customers..." and their quality mission statement pursues "customers for life" by establishing a "deep emotional connection" through a wide range of "products, services and experiences."[3]

1 Campbell's. "Strategies for Success: Management Strategy and Analysis." Accessed June 11, 2013. http://www.campbellsoupcompany.com/csr/pages/success/management-strategy-and-analysis.asp.

2 Starbucks. "Our Starbucks Mission Statement." Accessed June 11, 2013. http://www.starbucks.com/about-us/company-information/mission-statement.

3 Harley-Davidson. "This Is Where We Live Between Rides." Accessed June 11, 2013. http://www.harley-davidson.com/en_US/Content/Pages/Company/company.html.

As you discover the Assignment God has for you also think about writing down your life-mission statement. Our church has a mission statement I like very much. I have personally made it my own. The statement declares: "I am helping others see that God is more than they believe." It is a great statement, because it challenges a person to think about how capable God is to meet their needs and exceed what they can imagine when serving Him (see Ephesians 3:20-21). Sadly though, my experience has taught me that most people have a very low expectation of God. Comments like "I don't want to bother the man upstairs" or "My needs are not important enough to get heaven involved" often surface in conversation.

Having pastored a number of congregations over three decades, I have learned that most people do not really believe that God is going to provide them with a miracle. Our church staff has a saying: "People come to church with low expectations. We are never going to meet them there." Each time we get together at church, we ask God to do something extraordinary. Every aspect of fellowship in each of our worship services is laced with an attitude of excellence and a high expectation for God's presence to be manifested. We want the Spirit to become noticeable to all who attend. I want people who walk in with low expectations to walk out saying: "Wow! I have never been in a church like that before. It sure doesn't look like my grandma's church." That is our mission statement:

"We are helping others see that God is more than they believe."

THE MAD DASH COUNTDOWN

Discovering your Assignment from God cannot be put off. I urge you to simply start, somewhere, today. If you have not done so, a good start is at the Cross. From the Cross, find a person you respect as being a success and ask that person to help you discover what your unique purpose is in the Kingdom. Remember: never was there a winner who was not a beginner; never was there a winner who was not first a sinner.

Most translations are kind when they interpret the final part of David's life. Even the *New King James Version* says, "David fell asleep" (see Acts 13:36). If you look at that verse in the literal Greek you can interrupt it like this: "David flat died." One of these days we are all going to flat die. The skinny lady is going to take her place at the microphone and it is going to be over. What are you going to do about the mad dash between the dates?

The late Jim Rohn was labeled America's Foremost Business Philosopher and he was one of my favorite people. Jim followed Christ. Whenever you attended one of his seminars or read one of his books you realized how committed he was to God. Jim had a line that he always used, and I want you to think about it. He said: "Live your life in a way that you show up in someone else's testimony." Are people going to be talking about you in a positive light when you have found the exit door on the planet?

Remember, you are in the "mad dash between the dates" of your birth and death. The clock is ticking away. The greatest investment with the most satisfaction is putting your entire life—time, resources and talents—into advancing His name and sharing His love. One of the most memorable verses in the Bible says it all: "But seek first his kingdom and his righteousness, and all these things will be given to you" (Matthew 6:33).

PERSONAL QUEST

1. Who determines the number of days
   you live on earth—you or God?

2. Are funerals sad, peaceful, happy or
   meditative times for you?

3. Are people afraid to get old? Why or why not?

4. What practice or distraction squanders the
   most time in your life right now?

5. What practice or encouragement helps you to realize
   that your time on earth is precious in serving God?

6. How do you think God measures the worth of a man
   or woman's life? Does the Bible give us any clues?

***

"Train yourself to let go

of the things you fear to lose."

GEORGE LUCAS,
AMERICAN FILMMAKER, 1944–

CHAPTER 7

THE SIXTH SENSE— SUPERNATURAL 20/20 SIGHT

TODAY IN AMERICA it is quite common to not have a funeral when someone dies, but to have what is called a "Life Celebration." In some ways it does not seem right to mourn a life that has been well lived. Because, to be honest with you, the only person that can really celebrate is the person who has died and is already experiencing what is on the other side. Those who are still here are left to grieve and often the loss is too great to muster up much celebration. And since most have not been afforded the luxury of seeing the paranormal (that which is just outside our normal) we can only grieve. We are prisoners to our own five senses. If we could only get more glimpses into the Sixth Sense—the very real spiritual world—we would fare much better.

I have listened to hundreds of people who have had near-death experiences. There is a common thread that runs through all the accounts. I believe I am safe in saying that these are the top three post-NDE qualities that come through:

1. One no longer fears the prospect of dying.

2. Nearly everyone comes back and makes a change in the way they are presently living.

3. Nearly everyone wants to stay there. (If it were not for loved ones on this side, I am confident that everyone who has made peace with God would prefer staying in heaven.)

While Karen and I were pastors in Oceanside, California, we met a delightful elderly couple by the name of Charles and Nila Miller. Charles and Nila had been married for almost 60 years and had been pastors for a long, long time. When the time came for them to retire, they chose to retire near the Pacific Ocean in beautiful Southern California. For Charles and Nila, their golden years were akin to what the psalmist said, "LORD, you alone are my portion and my cup; you have made my lot secure. The boundary lines have fallen for me in pleasant places; surely I have a delightful inheritance" (Psalm 16:5-6).

If it were not for loved ones on this side, I am confident that everyone who has made peace with God would prefer staying in heaven.

One day, we received the sad news that Nila had passed away. While we rejoiced in the confidence that she was with her Savior, Jesus Christ, we still missed her greatly. We knew that the love shared by Charles and Nila ran very deep between them. For Charles, his grief was almost to the point of not wanting to carry on with his own life. Lifetime bonds that suddenly come to an end affect people profoundly—even the Taj Mahal (thought by many people to be the most beautiful building in the world) was built from the grief of a mourning husband.

Many weeks passed after Nila's death and then one day I received a call from Charles. He wanted me to come to his home and said that he had some things that he wanted to discuss with me. When I arrived at his home, Charles seemed a bit troubled. He cordially asked if I would like a glass of water. I could tell he was distracted as he showed me into the living room while not giving me a chance to answer his question. As he sat on the edge of the old leather chair, he wrung his hands as if hesitant to speak his mind. Slowly, he began to tell me how, during the time he had pastored a church, there had been a number of people who confided in him that something had happened to them that involved loved ones who had passed over to the other side. He said that he had heard quite a few stories, but had never really believed them until now.

He hesitated for a moment, as if giving me an opportunity to prepare for what he was about to tell me. "What's going on, Charles?" I asked cautiously. Charles looked at me through eyes that had seen many things over the years, searching my face to see if I could be trusted, and then he finally spoke.

"Something has happened recently that has changed my mind," explained Charles. "I now believe everything all those other people told me about their loved ones who had died." I was a little taken aback for a moment, because I knew Charles very well—he was an extremely intelligent man and not given to foolishness or triviality. Sensing that I might not be ready for what he was about to tell me, Charles slowly continued, "Nila has been coming to visit me. I have been so lonely for her, and she has been here. I can feel her run her fingers running through my hair. Just having her presence here is so comforting to me."

I was intrigued and couldn't help myself as I asked, "Has she said anything to you?"

"Yes." Charles answered in almost a whisper, "Nila tells me to get ready, because it is my time to join her. What do you think?"

I blinked a couple of times, and then could not help but smile as I replied, "Charles, I can't explain it, but I believe it. I believe it is time to get your things ready, it looks like you are about to go on a wonderful journey."

Relief washed over his face, and he appreciated the fact that I did not think he was crazy. "Thank you, Pastor Mike. Thank you." We had prayer before I left and that was the last time I was able to visit my friend. In just a few days, Charles succumbed to Nila's pleas to join him.

You may ask: Does that really happen? Can people from the other side come over and visit loved ones? Do we have the ability to talk to them? Are there angels hanging around us just outside of our reality? I am convinced there are…a lot of them. Allow me to suggest some readings on this matter.

AN INTELLIGENT READ

I have often heard it said, "As long as you are a leader then you need to be a reader." I am a voracious reader, and I enjoy encouraging others to read. There are three books that explore the paranormal that I think would be valuable for further study.

One of the best treatments of this subject was done by James Garlow and Keith Wall. Their book *Encountering Heaven and the Afterlife* is a collection of true stories of people who have had a glimpse of the world beyond. It is a good read. It is intelligently thought out and well researched, and reading it will stretch you. This book goes beyond what is considered the 'normal' experience of a NDE. There are accounts about people being visited by a loved one, a demon or angel. One of the most intriguing segments in the book—"Do You Believe in Ghosts?"—will challenge you. The authors write, "In spite of our best efforts at denial, mysterious encounters with otherworldly entities seem as common as ever."[4]

The Apostle Paul was always aware of the supernatural world around him. There is a connection between the temporal, physical form of this world and the eternal, spiritual content of the other.

> ••••••••••••••••••••••••••••
>
> *The authors write, "In spite of our best efforts at denial, mysterious encounters with otherworldly entities seem as common as ever."*
>
> ••••••••••••••••••••••••••••

Paul encouraged believers with these words: "Therefore we do not lose heart. Though outwardly we are wasting away, yet inwardly we are being renewed day by day. For our light and momentary troubles are achieving for us an eternal glory that far outweighs them all. So we fix our eyes not on what is seen, but on what is unseen since, is seen is temporary, but what is unseen is eternal (2 Corinthians 4:16-18). He had 20/20 spiritual vision, that Sixth Sense, to appreciate that life was more than physical reality, but involved a supernatural, spiritual world.

Garlow and Wall weave together a powerful arrangement of material that resonates with Scripture. Their exploration of the subject asks and addresses many nagging questions people have about the afterlife.

---

4 James Garlow, and Keith Wall, *Encountering Heaven and the Afterlife*, (Bloomington, Bethany House Publishers, 2010), 7.

A CONVERTED SKEPTIC

Dr. Mary C. Neal recently captured my attention when I read her book titled *To Heaven and Back. A Doctor's Extraordinary Account of Her Death, Heaven, Angels and Life Again*. Dr. Neal is the former director of spine surgery at the University of Southern California and is the founding partner of Orthopedic Associates of Jackson Hole, WY. She is highly educated and highly respected, and her book is a must read.

Dr. Neal is by nature a scientist and was taught to be a healthy skeptic. She recognizes that not everything we hear and see is factual or even interpreted logically. Yet her skepticism about an afterlife was radically altered when she had a kayak accident in Chile. She barely survived the ordeal, and came back with some interesting things she saw on the other side. At one point she said, "I am analytical, scientific and skeptical by nature and by training. I'm not sure I would believe all the events of my life's story to be true if I had not personally lived each day of them. ...I do know that millions of people are in dire need of God and experiencing His presence, and accepting the truth of His promises."[5]

Dr. Neal's transformation from skeptic to sensible believer in the supernatural and afterlife is moving. Below is a segment from her personal account that is quite thought provoking.

---

5 Mary C. Neal, M.D., *To Heaven and Back*, (Colorado Springs, Waterbrook Press 2012), 207.

One day after I had recovered enough to return to my medical practice, a woman I knew arrived at my office without an appointment. She knew it was my busiest day of the work week, but she insisted on speaking with me. Now, to understand this part of the story, you must understand our shared history. Shortly after I began my medical practice in Wyoming, this woman's husband had come to me for care. He underwent a major surgery, which I performed, and had no difficulties. His hospital course after surgery was entirely uncomplicated; he felt great and by the third day, I was beginning to plan his discharge from the hospital.

Unbeknownst to me, my patient and his wife had visited with their Latter-Day Saints bishop prior to this surgery and had received blessings from him. He had told my patient's wife that she would have to give up the thing that she loved the most. He told my patient that God was very pleased with him, that the veil between this world and the next would be very thin, and that he would be required to make a choice.

Before surgery, my patient and his wife had discussed together their interpretation of these blessings. They had concluded that my patient would have to choose between continued life on earth or physical death. They were both spiritually devoted and knew that my patient would choose God. On the fourth day after his surgery, my patient suddenly dropped dead while in the bathroom. His wife later told me that throughout the day of his passing, her husband had been speaking with angels who he said were in the room with them. He kept asking her if she could see them and was disappointed that she couldn't. He told her how much he loved and valued her as a wife, but that he had to go with the angels and that he would visit her.

Now back to the story. Given this background, and the fact that she had driven several hours to see me, I could not refuse her request for a bit of my time. We sat in the outdoor courtyard and she apologized profusely for interrupting my day, but she had something of great importance to tell me. She was very worried that something terrible was about to happen to me, and she felt like she needed to warn me. She told me that in the time since her husband's death, his spirit would occasionally visit their home and give her guidance.

She told me that in the time since her husband's death, his spirit would occasionally visit their home and give her guidance.

She had not seen him for many months, but he had come into her dreams the day before she drove to my office.

During this visitation, her husband had been excited and jubilant. He told her that I had been in a terrible accident and that he had asked the heavenly Father if he could be one of those sent to save me. As he described it to her, his request had been honored and he was so pleased to have been able to walk beside me and lift me up during that time.

His wife had known nothing of my boating accident in Chile, but she was able to give details of the scene that were known only to those who were present. After she completed her story and added her plea that I be careful, I told her the story of my accident. Although she was startled by the past tense of my story, she was not shocked by the story itself, as her husband had already told her many of the same details."[6]

Dr. Neal quotes a *Newsweek* article titled "In Search of the Sacred" (November 1994) and observed that twenty percent of Americans have had a revelation from God in the past year and thirteen percent have seen or sensed the presence of angels.

As a final thought, Dr. Neal said: "Many have said my experience is remarkable. Perhaps it is. What I find more remarkable, however, is how readily many people in our society believe outlandish and unsubstantiated urban myths and conspiracies (Pop Rocks and Coke, JFK assassination conspiracy, AIDS is man-made, etc.), yet disregard the thousands of personal and consistent testimonies of miracles and near-death experiences from people throughout all cultures and religions."[7]

PAYING ATTENTION TO GOD'S NUDGE

In my previous book *The God Nudge,* I wanted to help people see what is going on in heaven. In the church I pastor in Central

6 Mary C. Neal, M.D., *To Heaven and Back,* (Colorado Springs, WaterBrook Press, 2012), 197-201
7 Neal, 205.

California, I had the congregation perform the following exercise. I set up a few telephones to receive text messages during the church service and asked the question: "What do you think is going on in heaven?" Hundreds of people texted me back by the end of four services. Regrettably, there was not a single person who texted back with the answer I was hoping to see.

We received numerous answers one would expect to such a question, including statements like "people are reuniting with loved ones" or "people are engaged in worshipping God." One responder said, "No one is crying and no one is sick." While these are all correct answers, no one offered the answer I was hoping to see: "staff meetings."

That may sound odd to you, but I believe they are having staff meetings in heaven all the time. In Isaiah 6:8, the prophet is caught up in the spirit and has captured a vision of heaven. He peers upward and God is asking questions. "Whom shall I send? And who will go for us?" Sensing the urgency of the questions from his Lord, Isaiah answered: "Here am I. Send me!" Isaiah was able to drop in on a staff meeting conducted by God Himself.

Another case which illustrates this is found in 2 Chronicles 18. One of Israel's most evil rulers was King Ahab. At the close of his reign, King Ahab had talked King Jehoshaphat of Judah into going to battle against Ramoth Gilead. Before they left, Ahab brought together 400 prophets to ask them if they should go into battle. They all said, "Attack Ramoth Gilead and be victorious…for the Lord will give it into the king's hand" (v.11). However, King Jehoshaphat was known to be a man who was in tune with God on a regular basis. Ahab's prophets followed the god Baal while Jehoshaphat followed the one true God and he asked: "Is there no longer a prophet of the Lord here whom we can inquire of?" (v.6).

Ahab reluctantly tells Jehoshaphat about one prophet named Micaiah. This prophet of the Lord is hardly King Ahab's favorite because Micaiah always foretold bad things about Ahab and Israel. Nevertheless Jehoshaphat was insistent to hear God's counsel and Ahab had Macaiah brought up before them. Imagine, the one man who King Ahab does not want to hear from was now advising Jehoshaphat on going into battle.

> Micaiah said: "I saw the LORD sitting on his throne with all the multitudes of heaven standing on his right and on his left. And the LORD said, 'Who will entice Ahab king of Israel into attacking Ramoth Gilead and going to his death there?' One suggested this, and another that. Finally, a spirit came forward, stood before the LORD and said, 'I will entice him.' 'By what means?' the LORD asked. 'I will go and be a deceiving spirit in the mouths of all his prophets,' he said. 'You will succeed in enticing him,' said the LORD, 'Go and do it.'" (vv. 18-21).

They were having a staff meeting in heaven.

I make the comment in *The God Nudge* that "millions of prayers are coming off the planet each day. Heaven is having trouble finding people who can deliver the answer to those prayers. God showed up in Moses' day and everyone was freaked out. Jesus is not coming back until the end of time. Anytime an angel shows up in the Bible, people want to run and hide." Yet, God's plan is that we become His ambassadors on the earth… that we be attentive to what is happening in the staff meetings in heaven and act when we sense a God Nudge.

Earthly prayers have certainly attracted heaven's attention and heaven is now trying to get our attention. I would contend that angels, who are messengers from God, are consistently moving about the earth trying to get us involved in what concerns heaven. Many believers could be more involved in the supernatural side of life if they only made themselves more available. I promise this: if you ask God to use you with what concerns Him, He will.

The Apostle Paul understood how important it was to know God's will and be sensitive to how He wants to use us each day. When he wrote to the Philippians, Paul said: "And this is my prayer: that your love may abound more and more in knowledge and depth of insight, so that you may be able to discern what is best and may be pure and blameless for the day of Christ, filled with the fruit of righteousness that comes through Jesus Christ—to the glory and praise of God" (Philippians 1:9-11).

Are you getting the staff meeting memos from heaven? Are you listening to what God is prompting you to do today...right now? I inform heaven on a daily basis that I am a candidate to be used in the God Nudge. It is my prayer that you as well, will be one of heaven's 'go-to' people.

LIVING BEYOND YOUR FORM

There is a verse in the Bible that will transform your thinking if you allow it to: "And do not be conformed to this world, but be transformed by the renewing of your mind, that you may prove what is that good and acceptable and perfect will of God" (Romans 12:2, *NKJV*).

There are words in this passage of Scripture that I want to draw to your attention and understanding. The apostle says: "Do not be conformed to this world." If we take the word 'conformed' and split it up, we get CON-FORM-ED. "Con" appears as a prefix to words like *con*vict, *con*fined, *con*strict or *con*ceal. Paul is saying that we are not to be conformed, constrained or constricted by our natural physical form.

If you split the word 'transformation' into parts such as TRANS-FORM-A-TION, the middle word 'form' identifies you...the physical you and includes your physiological self. If you break us down as human beings into a pile of flesh, our form of bones, skin, toenails, blood vessels and arteries would not be much different from that of a pig. What I want to see is that there is something deeper that is not seen in the physical surface of things...I am talking about the spirit inside of you.

The real you is ninety-nine percent invisible! The real you is something beyond form. When you live exclusively by form, you live in a world of limitations. Think about those limits... you can only lift a certain amount of weight, you can only run so fast, and you can only work so hard. I encourage you to discover life outside of your physical form. Join thousands of others who have found out how to live life by their spirit and their imaginations.

Consider the part of you without physical limits. There is no limit to your ability to think. Can you imagine yourself doing anything? Can you imagine a great relationship with your spouse? You are experiencing life in the dimension that transcends your form. I believe everyone can experience life in the Spirit if they will allow themselves to get outside their five senses and tap into the jet stream of God.

Our mind is a powerful tool; it is capable of transcending form. The sky is the limit for those who have learned to tap into their Sixth Sense. Be aware as to when God is nudging you to do His good will and to see a larger spiritual picture. Learn to tap into a life that transcends the five senses—to empower the spiritual being within. It is an abundant life we are called to live as followers of Christ.

SPIRITUAL SIGHT BRINGS PRIORITY CHANGES

The more we see beyond the physical, temporal form of this world and recognize the spiritual—the Sixth Sense—we will see our everyday priorities change. Hungering for God's Presence and being aware of the supernatural working of God's Spirit at home, work and church is a major game-changer. I like the Apostle Paul's exhortation to believers to get their priorities into the unseen spiritual world and to store up the wealth that is eternal.

> *The more we see beyond the physical, temporal form of this world and recognize the spiritual—the Sixth Sense—we will see our everyday priorities change.*

He wanted them to have excellent spiritual 20/20 eyesight. "Therefore we do not lose heart. Though outwardly we are wasting away, yet inwardly we are being renewed day by day. For our light and momentary troubles are achieving for us an eternal glory that far outweighs them all. So we fix our eyes not on what is seen, but on what is unseen, since what is seen is temporary, but what is unseen is eternal" (2 Corinthians 4:16-18).

PERSONAL QUEST

1. Do you think people are afraid of the

   supernatural? If so why or why not?

2. What distracts you from thinking about what is eternal?

3. Is there anything in this physical world that has value?

4. How does God personally nudge you to do His will?

5. What single practice or change can you introduce

   into your life to think and be more aware of a

   spiritual world and God's supernatural power?

***

"To appreciate heaven well,

it's good for a person to have

some fifteen minutes of hell."

WILL CARLETON,
AMERICAN POET, 1845-1912

CHAPTER 8

I KNOW FIVE PEOPLE WHO WENT TO HELL—THREE ARE STILL THERE...

PEOPLE OFTEN SHY AWAY from any discussion about hell. It is an uncomfortable topic that is not talked about too much anymore. Keep reading…because people really do go to hell. I have read the Bible between 25-30 times and most of you know…it is not a small book. Contained within the pages of the Bible are the four most horrible words that were ever spoken. Those words came from the lips of Jesus. "And everyone who speaks a word against the Son of Man will be forgiven, but anyone who blasphemes against the Holy Spirit *will not be forgiven*" (Luke 12:10, author emphasis).

God is very tolerant of us. He knows that we make mistakes time and time again, and He is very willing to forgive us. However,

He does have His limits and when we exceed His patience we enter into judgment and there are plenty of examples to study.

KORAH'S REBELLION: GOD HAS LIMITS

Moses was a great leader. He brought the Israelites out of slavery in Egypt, and guided them through the desert to the Promised Land. Even though they were headed to the land of "milk and honey," it was a far cry from desert living. A destination that should have taken less than a week to reach ended up as a forty-year journey.

You can imagine the difficulty of wandering around in a hot desert with over a million people. One day, led by a man named Korah, the Israelites had grown grumpy over Moses (see Numbers 16). They accused him of not being led by God. This was a serious offense in the eyes of the Lord and prompted Him to kill 250 grumbling Israelites. They could not be forgiven for what they had done. These were not people from the mafia or some drug cartel. These were the noble and famous men among the Israelites. God was fed up with their grumbling, and called them to account. On that fateful day, these Israelites found out that speaking against a servant of God was costly. If God expressed such fury over His earthly servant, you can imagine the enormous seriousness when someone blasphemes the Holy Spirit and Jesus says it will not be forgiven

To be sure, each of us has to remember that we will be called to account one day before the Lord. The Bible is packed with stories of judgment that befell unrepentant rebels, and it is important to understand that God is longsuffering and patient, but He does bring everyone to a full accounting of deeds. In the end, either you can let God pay the bill of judgment through the work of His Son Jesus on the Cross who died for your sins or you can pay the bill of your sins yourself. "For the wages of sin is death, but the gift of God is eternal life in Christ Jesus our Lord (Romans 6:23).

When your bill comes due who will pay for your sin? You can pay for it or you can accept God's payment in sending His Son for you.

BELSHAZZAR: NO ONE MOCKS GOD

In Daniel, chapter 5, a king by the name of Belshazzar crossed the line of tolerance with God. Verses 1-4 set the scene for what was about to happen.

> "King Belshazzar gave a great banquet for a thousand of his nobles and drank wine with them. While Belshazzar was drinking his wine, he gave orders to bring in the gold and silver goblets that Nebuchadnezzar his father had taken from the temple in Jerusalem, so that the king and his nobles, his wives and his concubines might drink

from them. So they brought in the gold goblets that had been taken from the temple of God in Jerusalem, and the king and his nobles, his wives and his concubines drank from them. As they drank the wine, they praised the gods of gold and silver, of bronze, iron, wood and stone" (Daniel 5:1-7).

Drinking from these goblets was a brazen act of arrogance, because the items had been dedicated to the Lord by the Jewish temple priests before Jerusalem had fallen to the Babylonians. Bottom line: Belshazzar was mocking God. He was showing a crude disrespect for the Almighty. The next part of the story tells us that "Suddenly the fingers of a human hand appeared and wrote on the plaster of the wall, near the lampstand in the royal palace. The king watched the hand as it wrote. His face turned pale and he was so frightened that his legs became weak and his knees were knocking" (vv. 5-6).

Talk about being terrified! I think my knees would be knocking too if I saw a huge hand writing words on a wall! Suffice it to say that none of the king's enchanters or astrologers could translate what was written, but Daniel could. When Daniel, who had been sitting in prison, was called before the king, he decided to take the time to give the king a little history lesson, reminding him of the not-so-pleasant lessons that 'Neb' his grandfather had learned (see Daniel 5:18-21).

Daniel then says, "But you, Belshazzar, his son, have not humbled yourself, though you knew all this. Instead, you have set yourself up against the Lord of heaven. You had the goblets from his temple brought to you, and you and your nobles, your wives and your concubines drank wine from them. You praised the gods of silver and gold, of bronze, iron, wood and stone, which cannot see or hear or understand. But you did not honor the God who holds in his hand your life and all your ways. Therefore he sent the hand that wrote the inscription" (vv. 22-24).

He had been weighed and found short and the kingdom would be broken up and given to others (see vv. 25-28). Within 24 hours Belshazzar was dead. No one mocks God.

Ouch. Daniel didn't hold anything back.

Now Daniel read the four words "MENE MENE TEKEL PARSIN" that had been etched into the walls. The news was as bad as it gets...God told Belshazzar his days had been numbered and were to be brought to an end. He had been weighed and found short and the kingdom would be broken up and given to others (see vv. 25-28). Within 24 hours Belshazzar was dead.

No one mocks God.

KING AGRIPPA: "ALMOST" IS NOT ENOUGH

One of the saddest stories of sinning away the day of grace is in Acts, chapter 26. The Apostle Paul is held by the Roman authorities when he gets an audience with King Agrippa. Paul knows that King Agrippa is a Jew who is familiar with Jewish laws. Therefore, Paul appeals to a kinship with Agrippa by sharing about their Jewish heritage, and then goes on to explain his conversion.

> "While thus occupied, as I journeyed to Damascus with authority and commission from the chief priests, at midday, O king, along the road I saw a light from heaven, brighter than the sun, shining around me and those who journeyed with me. And when we all had fallen to the ground, I heard a voice speaking to me and saying in the Hebrew language, 'Saul, Saul, why are you persecuting Me? It is hard for you to kick against the goads.' So I said, 'Who are You, Lord?' And He said, 'I am Jesus, whom you are persecuting. But rise and stand on your feet; for I have appeared to you for this purpose, to make you a minister and a witness both of the things which you have seen and of the things which I will yet reveal to you. I will deliver you from the Jewish people, as well as from the Gentiles, to whom I now send you, to open their eyes, in order to turn them from darkness to light, and from the power of Satan to God, that they may receive forgiveness of sins and an inheritance among those who are sanctified by faith in Me'" (Acts 26:12-18 *NKJV*).

This whole time, Paul keeps his eyes locked on King Agrippa's eyes, not paying attention to the Roman governor Festus or the rest of the crowd in attendance. Paul makes a final appeal:

> "Therefore, King Agrippa, I was not disobedient to the heavenly vision, but declared first to those in Damascus and in Jerusalem, and throughout all the region of Judea, and then to the Gentiles, that they should repent, turn to God, and do works befitting repentance. For these reasons the Jews seized me in the temple and tried to kill me. Therefore, having obtained help from God, to this day I stand, witnessing both to small and great, saying no other things than those which the prophets and Moses said would come—that the Christ would suffer, that He would be the first to rise from the dead, and would proclaim light to the Jewish people and to the Gentiles" (Acts 26:19-23, *NKJV*).

At this point, Festus (who does not understand everything Paul is talking about) decides to divert Agrippa's attention from Paul. Felix shouts that Paul is mad! Felix says to Paul, "your great learning is driving you insane!" Festus knows Paul was bred to be a Pharisee—a top-notch religious scholar.

Anyone who is passionate for the Lord's Kingdom is assaulted with the line—"You are crazy!"

Festus criticizes Paul in the same way religious leaders stigmatized John the Baptist and Jesus Christ. Anyone who is passionate for the Lord's Kingdom is assaulted with the line—"You are crazy!"

Paul challenges Festus by stating that he speaks the words of truth and reason as told by the prophets. Then, Paul does something unprecedented: He asks King Agrippa a question and then answers his own question before the king can! "King Agrippa, do you believe the prophets? I know that you believe" (v. 28a). It is at this point that King Agrippa utters some of the most heartbreaking words recorded..."Paul, you almost persuade me to become a Christian" (v. 28b).

Almost? Almost! Almost...not enough.

A YOUNG LADY NAMED KATIE

Some time back I had the privilege of hearing Rev. J. Harold Smith—a powerful evangelist. He has since passed away. There are not many people like Rev. Smith—a man who loved winning people to Jesus. Some say Rev. Smith that led more people to Jesus in his lifetime than anyone else. He averaged bringing four people to Christ a day. He preached a message titled "Sinning Away Your Day of Grace"[8] which he took from the Book of Proverbs: "He who, being often reproved, hardens his neck shall suddenly be destroyed—and that without remedy" (Proverbs 29:1, *AMP*).

It was a very difficult message to hear. He told about how people that he personally knew had crossed the line with God

8 Fundamental Baptist Sermons Archive, "God's Three Deadlines." Audio Sermon, Accessed June 2013. http://fundamentalbaptistsermons.net/sermons165.htm.

and sinned away their day of grace. Having been acquainted with some people who went to hell, Rev. Smith would occasionally mention a number of poetic couplets that originate from a poem entitled "The Hidden Line (The Destiny of Men)" written by the 19th century biblical scholar Joseph Addison Alexander:

> *There is a time, we know not when, a point we know not where,*
> *That marks the destiny of men to glory or despair.*
> *There is a line by us unseen, that crosses every path;*
> *The hidden boundary between God's patience and his wrath[9]*

One of the people Rev. Smith knew was a 14-year-old girl named Katie. While preaching a sermon one evening, he felt impressed by the Holy Spirit to come off the platform and speak to a young girl sitting in a pew. He asked, "Young lady have you ever thought about giving your heart to Jesus."

She replied, "Sometimes."

Harold then asked, "If you knew that you were going to die by midnight tonight, would you let me pray with you?"

The girl said, "My Mom and Dad asked me the same question, and I told them 'No', so I'm telling you the same thing...No."

Rev. Smith tried his best to lead Katie to Christ that night, but she refused. She told him that she was young and had plenty of time. After church Katie and her family filled up the car with

9 Cavaliers Only Archive, "The Hidden Line (The Destiny of Men)." Accessed June 10, 2013. http://www.cavaliersonly.com/poetry_by_christian_poets_of_the_past/the_hidden_line_the_destiny_of_men_by_joseph_addison_alexander.

gas and headed home. While traveling they were hit by a drunk driver who had three companions with him.

Katie's family car rolled across the road and down a hill. Her mom was thrown out of the car on the first roll; her dad was thrown out on the second roll. When the car came to a rest, Katie was pinned in the back seat. As the intoxicated men scrambled out of their car, they began to make their way up the incline to where Katie was trapped. One of the disoriented men stumbled about and lit up a cigarette to calm his nerves, and without thinking threw the match on the ground. Gasoline from Katie's car had already run down the hill and when the match hit the ground a ribbon of fire ran up the road. Immediately, Katie and the car she was trapped in were engulfed in flames.

One witness said: "We tried to get the girl unpinned in the backseat. We worked with it five minutes and then saw a flash of lightning. We knew we had to abandon her. I will never forget what I heard the next few minutes."

Another witness to the crash said Katie cried out, "'Daddy, Momma, I am going to hell. I wish I had listened to Preacher Smith!' Katie's mom got as close as she could to the car, and said: 'Katie, you are going to die, pray and ask Jesus to save you.' 'Momma, I can't pray.' She slipped into eternity. And her last recorded words were: 'I'm damned Momma.'"[10]

10 Fundamental Baptist Sermons Archive, "God's Three Deadlines," Accessed June 2013,

FARMER JOHN

Rev. J. Harold Smith said he personally knew of 20 people who crossed the line with God and sinned away their day of grace. The most chilling story involved a wealthy farmer who attended a service where Rev. Smith had been speaking as part of a crusade led by Pastor Roberts. The account is included in his message entitled "God's Three Deadlines."[11]

John the farmer was the richest man in town. He owned a peach orchard. One evening, John and his family came into the church. The preacher asked him to come to Christ, but John just shook his head no and said: "Preacher I can't. That was a good sermon, but I am making a deal next Wednesday that is going to make me $25,000." (During the Depression, that was like half a million dollars.) John went on to say, "If I got saved I would have to call off the deal because it is crooked."

"So you are placing a $25,000 price tag on your soul" Rev. Smith replied.

John smirked, "I never looked at it like that."

On Tuesday, at two a.m., Pastor Roberts received a call from John's wife. "You have to come because John is sick." As Pastor Roberts reached their home he could hear John screaming, "Don't let him have me."

"John, this it Pastor Roberts, there is no one here to get you."

http://fundamentalbaptistsermons.net/sermons165.htm
11 Radio Bible Hour, "God's Three Deadlines." Accessed June 2013. SRVideo1. http://www.radiobiblehour.org

"Don't' you see him Preacher? He's coming up the drive... now he's coming in the front door...look! He's in my bedroom. He's wrapping that chain around my feet and my neck. He's got me preacher...I'm going to hell, preacher!"

TYRONE'S ROADSIDE ACCIDENT

Tyrone Williams was a young man with a turbulent and painful childhood that propelled him into a life of crime and drug addiction.

One night after a long trip, Tyrone, his girlfriend Shavonna and her two-year-old son, drove southbound on a winding section of the I-5 Freeway not far from Redding, California Both Tyrone and Shavonna were exhausted, but both decided to continue the drive to Sacramento. Tyrone quickly fell asleep on the passenger side as Shavonna took her turn to drive. Not long after, Tyrone was abruptly awakened. Shavonna had dozed off. The car was swerving side to side over a bumpy road. Even as Tyrone attempted to take hold of the driver's wheel, Shavonna also woke up and instinctively hit the brakes. The front tire blew out and the car began to tumble into the middle of a grassy divider between the northbound and southbound lanes of traffic. Tyrone was thrown about inside the vehicle. He blacked out. The turbulence in the car catapulted him through the windshield. His hand and lower arm were severed. His body was thrown into a nearby watery ditch.

When the car came to a rest, Shavonna frantically called out Tyrone's name. She had a broken nose and the baby was bleeding from the head. A young Hispanic man named Aruba come to her aid. Normally he took an alternate freeway—Hwy 101—to get to Oregon, but this time he happened to be on the I-5 Freeway. Aruba said there was a man standing behind Shavonna as she desperately cried out for Tyrone. The stranger pointed Aruba toward where the watery ditch was located and merely said, "He's in there."

Aruba hopped over a barb-wired fence and eventually pulled Tyrone's body from a murky, 7-ft. deep, watery grave. Neither breathing nor conscious from the injuries, the arriving paramedics did CPR in an effort to revive him while attending to his blood loss. Tyrone records what happens next:

> People were working on me, and trying to keep me calm, as well as keep me alive until help came. I passed out again; I woke up to being tied down in a helicopter. While my eyes were closed, I heard paramedics saying, "Just hang in there, you're going to be alright. Just hang in there. Come on, you got to hang in there with us. Don't go! Don't! Just hang in there." I felt the cold wind, and while I was in the air, I heard the helicopter, the propellers, the noise, as it was lifting up off of the ground, and we flew off. As they put the mask over my face, I breathe once and then twice, and I was out again.

At this point the supernatural world came into view. Once my body went into the water, my spirit separated from my body instantly. The paramedics sort-of called me back when they were given me CPR, but I was still crossed over. When I was thrown into the water, the world flipped upside down and my spirit left my flesh. In the spirit it was still me, though. I popped up out of the water, and I was looking around, and I notice I was underground. I was in a big, giant cave. The water, the taste, the smell, what I heard and saw, and what I touched, everything was intensified ten times. The water was black and slimy; the smell was like stale, old food, and the decay of flesh. I heard the screams of people, as if they were yelling for help from pain and torment.[12]

Tyrone says he spent five days in the underworld trying to return to his own. When he did return only minutes had passed on earth. The trauma from what he witnessed on the other side greatly affected Tyrone. He finally understood how real the physical and spiritual worlds were connected. He concludes:

"God is turning me to many new blessings, and the Holy Spirit has given me many new gifts that, initially, I really didn't know how deal with, handle, or control. Everything just hit me at once, and I was so scared lying in that hospital bed. I think the first time God touched me was about a week after I was up and the doctors had taken the tubes out of my body. I was sitting

---

12 Free CD Tracts, "Tyrone Went to Hell: The Tyrone Williams Story" Index Page. Accessed June 10, 2013 http://www.freecdtracts.com/testimony/tyrone_williams.htm.

there and He touched me and it all hit me again. This time I started crying. I broke down, and I picked up the telephone and called my grandmother. I said, "Grandmother, I'm ready." She said, "Repeat after me," and we said the sinner's prayer."[13]

Since the accident, Tyrone has gone on to become a minister, sharing his testimony with everyone he meets of how God rescued him from hell so that he can tell others that they, too, can be rescued and have a home in heaven with God.

MATT'S RANDOM DRIVE-BY SHOOTING

Matt was a businessman in his 20s living in Atlanta, Georgia. He was pursuing the American dream. His goal in life was to work hard so that he would be able to purchase a house on the lake. One evening, he walked out in front of a restaurant where he had just finished dinner and waited for the taxi that he had called to pick him up. He was enjoying the scenery around him while he waited for the taxi to arrive.

As he stood there, he heard a car engine revving, tires squealing, as a car came down the street. Without time to react, Matt heard the unmistakable sound of gunfire. Someone in the car was shooting a 9-mm gun...blanketing the building and Matt with a hail of bullets. The sensation of being hit by a bullet through the head was, for Matt, like someone running a hot poker through his

13 http://www.freecdtracts.com/testimony/tyrone_williams.htm.

skull. He crumpled to the ground. A pool of blood began to form; darkness covered his eyes. Later, Matt would recount the feeling as akin to blank ink being poured over his eyesight. He had a bullet lodged in the right side of his brain.[14]

Matt died almost as fast as it took for him to hit the ground. Matt says he was instantly transferred from one dimension to another. When the ambulance arrived, they hurried him to the ER. While paramedics worked to resuscitate him, Matt felt himself being dropped into a cell in hell—his arms and legs were shackled—and he was stretched over a deep, dark abyss.

He could smell the gray smoke as it billowed up and swirled around him from the pit below. His clothes had been stripped away. He could feel the rising heat from the glowing embers in the pit. He says, "I could hear screams, and very low guttural sounds. I couldn't understand the screams, but could feel pure evil. One thing I do know: This place was a place of no hope, no dreams and no desires."

Time was non-existent in hell. Matt pondered his situation: "Something eternal was happening to me. I was being tortured, but the fear and dread added to it was the real torture. I had never experienced anything even close to being as fearful as this. Pure evil had horrified me and I could tell that there was no way out."

---

14 Nancy Botsford, "A Day in Hell" (Mustang, Oklahoma; Tate Publishing & Enterprises, LLC, 2010), 18-19.

Matt had been married for some time, but in the cell he could not recall any memories of his wife. Love did not belong in the cell where he was being kept. "I finally realized," said Matt, "this is what happens when you die and go to hell."

Matt further records, "I was being kept. I couldn't move to the left or right. I had the feeling of being confined forever. While I am experiencing this, an incredible evil was pressing in on me—then, something begins to happen. I see something poking through the upper right hand corner of where I was being confined. It looked as if someone one was trying to push their index finger into a black plastic bag." Matthew then describes that he saw a hand...it was an aged hand, but it was also translucent. A bright light accompanied the hand and it was his first feeling of hope. "As the hand was descending, I felt this was a good thing happening to me. I thought, 'Maybe I will be rescued.'"

Matt says he heard the sound of stringed instruments next. "Music began to fill the air unlike any music I had ever heard or could describe. It was multiple instruments all making the most beautiful music. Immediately, the hand reaches through in order to rescue me. When the hand got through the darkness, the shackles around my wrists legs disappeared. I no longer had the feeling of being confined. All feelings of being constrained had left. I then began to hear a voice. This was not a normal voice.

This was the voice of rushing mighty water saying to me: 'It's not your time.'"

As Matt struggled in the underworld, his wife Nancy had her hands full in the ER. Dead for 4 minutes, the multiple electrical shocks had failed to revive Matt. His organs began to shut down. Medical personnel asked Nancy to sign the release form so they could harvest Matt's remaining organs. Nancy refused. Instead she knelt beside the bed where Matt was laying and asked God to bring her husband back. Heaven heard her request and the doctors found a pulse. Matt was resuscitated but remained in a deep coma. Weeks passed and Nancy continued to ask God to restore her husband, and then on the 27th day, Matt woke from his coma in a hospital room lined with 'Get Well' cards.

Matt survived his ordeal, but for two long years remained in rehabilitation. He made good progress even with a hole in his neck where the paramedic had made a tracheotomy. The doctors had agreed to leave the bullet lodged in Matt's brain fearing that any removal would cost him his life. More than 20 years later, he is alive and partially paralyzed on his left side.

Matt is quick to address why he experienced hell. "I am not quite sure but it makes me want to tell everyone: hell is a real place. I've seen the bad side and based on my choices today I am not going to hell anymore." Matt went on to say, "There are only two places you can spend eternity: Hell…where I went; or heaven…where I am now going. I am not afraid to die now. And the reason: I know exactly where I am going."[15]

SOMEONE IS PRAYING FOR YOU

The near-death experiences of Matt and Tyrone are compelling to read, but it is easy to overlook something they both shared. Both men had persistent and heartfelt prayers from friends and family. Do you ever wonder why some people are allowed to come back from hell and others never return? Many people I have listened to over the years allude to someone topside who was praying for them. Matt had a praying wife; Tyrone had a praying Grandmother. Don't ever give up on praying for your loved ones.

I am here today as a result of my family members not giving up on me when I was living a hellish lifestyle for years. It was their prayers, and the prayers of their church groups, that would not allow me to sin away my day of grace. Paul's exhortation to Timothy is meant for all of us.

> "I urge, then, first of all, that petitions, prayers, intercession and thanksgiving be made for all people—for kings and all those in authority, that we may live peaceful and quiet lives in all godliness and holiness. This is good, and pleases God our Savior, who wants all people to be saved and to come to a knowledge of the truth" (1 Timothy 2:1-4).

15 "I Survived Death and Beyond: Hell is Real." https://vimeo.com/23882051.

WHERE ARE ALL MY DEAD FRIENDS?

Many of the friends that I hung out with as a teenager did not change their lifestyles. Where are those childhood friends today? Many of them are dead. Robbie killed himself with a shotgun. To my knowledge he never made peace with God. Gary died in an automobile accident. He was a faithful attender at the Baptist Church and I would like to believe that he made it to heaven. John died in jail from sclerosis of the liver. He was headstrong and took as much as he could get out of life. It never mattered to him who he hurt. Occasionally he attended the Church of Christ congregation. I still wonder if Jesus Christ was made Lord of all in his life.

There are others: I cannot forget Larry who was killed in a pool hall incident. He had a tremendous heart, but bothered him that I would talk about God. I remember that as soon as I was born again, I went to tell Larry how he needed to be born again as well. He was deeply troubled in his spirit. He told me to never speak to him again about God. So, I didn't, until I performed his funeral.

My first love, Becky, died with the same disease that took Elvis Presley. She died at the same age as her mother. She was not very spiritual and eventually we broke up. Our lives took totally different paths. When I received a call that she had become ill I wanted to visit her, but she would not let anyone see her. She died too young.

So, again I ask...where are all my dead friends now? The truth is, I do not know. Where each one is right now is between them and God. Here is another question for you: where will you go when you die? Of course, that is also between you and God. Yet, you can make sure that heaven is your destination by accepting Jesus Christ as your personal Lord and Savior. I would like to give you a second chance to make your peace with God by having you say this prayer:

> *Lord Jesus, please forgive me of all my sins. I confess I am a sinner who needs a Savior. I believe Jesus you are the Savior, and I invite You to take over my life. Jesus, since You died for me, I am going to start living for You. I need Your help. Fill me with Your Holy Spirit and tell me what You want me to do with my life. Amen.*

Once you have prayed this prayer, look around where you live and find a good Bible-believing church. Begin to daily read God's Word—*The Holy Bible*—and ask the Lord to open your mind to His ways. You will find that God's been there all along for you. He has been waiting for you to have a conversation with Him. The Bible teaches us that He will never leave you or forsake you (see Hebrews 13:5). In this relationship, God is faithful even if we are the ones who often walk away from Him. I encourage you to live your life in a way that you will show up in someone else's testimony. Please know, I'll be praying for you!

PERSONAL QUEST

1. Do people who believe in heaven always believe in hell? Why or why not?

2. Do you think anyone is beyond the reach of God's redemption?

3. What does the Bible show us about God's feelings over sin?

4. What are some Bible passages that describe hell and heaven?

5. Why does the Bible carry an urgency to come to know God in a personal way?

"I can see how it might

be possible for a man

to look down upon the earth

and be an atheist,

but I cannot conceive

how he could look up

into the heavens and say

there is no God."

ABRAHAM LINCOLN,
16TH AMERICAN PRESIDENT, 1809-1865

CHAPTER 9

GOD'S GPS FOR FINDING ETERNAL LIFE

HOW DOES ONE AVOID living a wasted life? How does it happen that a person rejects or wanders away from God? Why are we rebellious? And how do we live a fulfilled life in the Lord because heaven and hell are real destinations? Like the new Global Positioning System (GPS) technology in cars that shows us how to find the right destination, we need God's GPS—the Word—to point the way to true life.

There is a verse in the New Testament that addresses sin. Jesus never really used the word "sinner" to describe people who were distant from God. "For the Son of Man came to seek and to save the lost" (Luke 19:10). Jesus looked at their lives and saw people wasting time and strength on temporary things here on earth. In Matthew, chapter 9, Jesus stands outside a crowd one day and spoke these words: "When He saw the crowds, He had compassion on them, because they were harassed and helpless, like sheep without a shepherd" (Matthew 9:36).

The Scripture says that Jesus was moved with compassion. It is easy to miss what really happened that day if you merely look at the English wording of the text. Let us pierce the surface of our language and look beneath at the original wording. The New Testament was written in Greek, and the Greek has a lot to say in this passage. Jesus was moved in the depth of His being—His inward parts—as described in the Greek word, *splagchizomai*. The best way to describe what He was feeling that day would be akin to what we feel after losing a loved one. Jesus' pain was heartfelt...it was at the core of His being.

> *Notice Jesus calls people who are not connected to Him as "lost" (see Luke 19:10; Matthew 18:11, NKJV) and not sinners.*

Notice Jesus calls people who are not connected to Him as "lost" (see Luke 19:10; Matthew 18:11 NKJV) and not sinners. The Greek word used for "lost" is *apollen*. That word can also be translated "waste." Jesus looked at the people and saw because they were without a mentor, they were living a wasted life. How tragic would it be to have come to the end of your days having lived a wasted life? It does not have to be that way at all. There is a passage in Scripture that is powerful to any of you still resisting God's invitation of salvation, and it is equally powerful to those of you who may have prayed the sinner's prayer in the previous chapter. Let me share God's word for you.

FOLLOWING IN THE STEPS OF THE WICKED

Psalm 1 is a powerful passage of Scripture. It shows how you can live for God or how you can get nailed to a cross like the thief that rejected Jesus on Calvary's hill. None of us want to end up getting nailed to a cross and heading into a Christ-less eternity. There is way to change it. There is a way to live for God. The psalmist has given us a roadmap in the Bible.

The psalmist writes,

"Blessed is the man who walks not in the counsel of the ungodly, nor stands in the path of sinners, nor sits in the seat of the scornful; but his delight is in the law of the LORD, and in His law he meditates day and night. He shall be like a tree planted by the rivers of water, that brings forth its fruit in its season, whose leaf also shall not wither; and whatever he does shall prosper. The ungodly are not so, but are like the chaff which the wind drives away. Therefore the ungodly shall not stand in the judgment, nor sinners in the congregation of the righteous. For the LORD knows the way of the righteous, but the way of the ungodly shall perish" (Psalm 1:1-6, *NKJV*).

The psalmist says from the first verse that we should not walk in the steps of the wicked. *The Holy Bible: New International Version* says, "Blessed is the one who does not walk in step with the wicked." Think back to a moment when you were a little child following after an adult, and you tried to use your chubby little legs to match their footprints—stride for stride. If you have chosen to follow someone who has wasted their life in sin, you will eventually grow up taking bigger and bigger steps in wasting your own life. You will forfeit your opportunity for a blessed life.

It is possible to be corrupted by the evil behavior of those we admire or envy. The wicked may give us a false sense of acceptance and identity. Little kids love to mimic, and teenagers go along with peer pressure, and adults often succumb to the hollow temptations of the world for power and status. In the Bible, Israel's King Ahab was influenced many times by his wife Jezebel who worshiped Baal and defied the Lord. Ahab's life ended miserably.

DO NOT TRAFFIC IN THE WAY OF SIN

Secondly, Psalm 1 points out this truth: "Don't stand in the way of sinners." It is almost as if you are standing at a bus station waiting on the bus to pick you up. If that is a bus station where sin is the main business of the day then you are standing in the pathway of sinners. Each day you and I are at a point of decision. Do I stand and be trafficked by sin or do I find a group of people who have not patterned their lives after sinful living?

Once I was standing on a street corner by myself in a foreign country, contemplating what I was going to eat. As I waited for the traffic to go by, I got this most unusual thought that I should try Ecstasy. I have never seen Ecstasy, but it is a drug that became common in the United States in the 1980s when 'Rave' parties were popular. From the research I have done, Ecstasy or 'E' is one of those drugs that can have damaging effects the very first time you use it. It is a powerful stimulant with hallucinogenic effects that releases a mass of serotonin from the brain. One report regarding global drug use estimated that as many as 25 million people have taken Ecstasy at some point in their lives.[16] In the U.S. alone, over 14 million people have taken the drug at some point in their lifetime, with about 1 million people trying it for the first time each year.[17]

When someone takes E, they will begin to experience the effects of the drug within about 15 minutes. Because of the effects that Ecstasy has on the pleasure or "reward" chemicals in the brain, users experience a sense of euphoria and well-being, a boost in energy, along with enhanced sensory perceptions. The effect usually lasts anywhere from 3-6 hours, depending on the

16 United Nations Office on Drug and Crime, "World Drug Report 2010" (Vienna, Austria; UN Publication Sales, 2010), 100.
17 "World Drug Report 2010," 124.

dosage and drug purity. However, when the user begins to come down off E, they feel tired and dehydrated. A person's short-term memory will suffer for a period of time as well as the appetite will disappear for 2-3 days, followed by 3-5 days of depression. Because of the undesirable physical and psychological side effects, many users will just simply take more of the drug, leading the way developing a full-blown addiction. Studies have also shown that serotonin levels can be affected for years after use of the drug. This affect can cause long-term depression, and even lead to suicide in some individuals.[18]

Now, I have been following Christ for years, but this day I was being visited by an evil spirit. It was not just a thought. It was a feeling that was far more compelling than usual. I thought: *I am standing in a pathway of sinners. This is where evil is trafficking!*

Most people do not understand what happens spiritually when we stand in the way of sinners. Jesus gave us an interesting insight to how evil spirits work. Since their success is banking on anonymity, you would not hear much about how the devil and his underlings work. "When an unclean spirit goes out of a man, he goes through dry places, seeking rest, and finds none. Then he says, 'I will return to my house from which I came.' And when he comes, he finds it empty, swept, and put in order. Then

18 "Ecstasy Side Effects." Accessed on June, 10, 2013. http://www.ecstasy.ws/e-side-effects.htm.

he goes and takes with him seven other spirits more wicked than himself, and they enter and dwell there; and the last state of that man is worse than the first. So shall it also be with this wicked generation" (Matthew 12:43-45, *NKJV*).

This passage teaches us that evil spirits like to traffic in dry places. When we are going about our daily lives without a hint of God, then we are living in dry places. We are the playground of the enemy. Not just one evil spirit, but the Bible says that seven other spirits accompanied their evil leader to use a person's life as a platform from which to operate wrongful acts. You cannot clean up your act on your own…you need God's help to do it.

You cannot clean up your act on your own…you need God's help to do it.

Also, without getting 'spooky' spiritual on you, it seems that in the Bible evil spirits do not do well with water. When a person is born again, one steps into a refreshing life and it is usually depicted as a watery experience. "Anyone who believes in me may come and drink! For the Scriptures declare, 'Rivers of living water will flow from his heart.'" (John 7:38 *NLT*).

John the Baptist pointed out to the crowds that "'I indeed baptize you with water; but One mightier than I is coming, whose sandal strap I am not worthy to loose. He will baptize you with the Holy Spirit and fire" (Luke 3:16, *NKJV*).

Even the Apostle John gives us an understanding here: "For an angel went down at a certain time into the pool and stirred up the water; then whoever stepped in first, after the stirring of the water, was made well of whatever disease he had" (John 5:4, NKJV).

The prophet Ezekiel saw water coming from God's holy place. "In my vision, the man brought me back to the entrance of the Temple. There I saw a stream flowing east from beneath the door of the Temple and passing to the right of the altar on its south side" (Ezekiel 47:1, *NLT*)

Let the waters of God's mercy and grace enter into your life. Do not stand around in the highway of sin. Otherwise, you will be pulled into foolishness and waste your life.

THE SEAT OF THE CYNICAL

The third thing to learn from Psalm 1 is that we should not "sit in the seat of scornful" people. When we sit with these individuals, we have ceased all movement towards God. It is so easy nowadays to become cynical about life and the things of God. If we allow our minds to go down that path we will find ourselves living in Negative Town. Nothing good happens in Negative Town. Everyone there is up to 'no good.' They will provide you with a lot of ideas on how to become a successful 'doer of no good.'

A friend of mine who is a minister recently travelled to South Africa. His traveling companion is also a pastor. One afternoon, they decided to stop at a restaurant and eat. As is their custom, they began to pray over the meal. Now this was not an ordinary meal prayer because they began to pray for the restaurant establishment as well. Their server was a young lady who happened to overhear their prayers for the restaurant. She walked up to them and shared, "I have need for prayer too." The two ministers prayed for her. The waitress then had the restaurant owner meet them, who also admitted his need for prayer!

At the next table were three ladies intently watching the 'prayer meeting' unfold in the restaurant. They began to mock: "You prayed for them, why don't you pray for us?" One of the ministers received a God nudge and felt impressed to tell her something that was specific about her and her husband. The lady confirmed he was right. He then went on to tell one of her companions, "And you are a backslidden child of God." This woman had a father who was a great man of prayer who pastored a church in Africa. Unlike her father, she had walked away from God, her family, and had landed in prison. What an amazing moment it was for her to run into two praying preachers—two men who simply decided to ask God to sanctify their food just before they ate it! Incredible!

This wayward lady had been sitting in the seat of the scornful. She had been hanging out with critical and negative people and it forfeited her blessings. If you live an entire life hanging around scornful people you can end up in hell just like the second thief on the cross. Dr. Mike Smalley has written an entire book on this subject entitled *Saved Soul Wasted Life.*[19]*

Dr. Smalley calls the second thief on the cross the most tragic man who ever lived. I think he is right. How can you spend six hours in the presence of the Creator of worlds and not have a life-changing experience? The thief who rejected Jesus had hardened his heart one-too-many times. Here he is on a cross with Jesus the Lord who created the earth, all its creatures, plant life, the oceans, and continents we call today North America, Australia, Europe, Africa, Asia and the island nations like New Zealand, Hawaii, Greenland and more. He is next to Jesus who called our world into being and he was too blind to see the Lord's love toward him. When it came to the dreadful end, the thief with the hard heart had no ability whatsoever to apply the claims of Christianity. He had been around the cynical, the scornful, and wasteful too long, and it left him bankrupt to see the wealth in salvation.

> *How can you spend six hours in the presence of the Creator of worlds and not have a life-changing experience?*

19 For more information on books by Dr. Smalley visit http://www.mikesmalley.com.

WAY OF THE RIGHTEOUS

Lastly, the psalmist stresses the importance to "meditate in God's Word day and night." Why?

There is power in how God's Spirit uses the Word. The power comes in cleaning out any ugly spirit that may have weaved itself into your lifestyle. Spending time in the Bible is like getting out of a shower. When you hear the Word, you have placed your spirit in the rub-a-dub-dub, bathtub of God. You need soap and water to clean your body, but the Word of God cleans out your mind. If you really want to get clean, begin reading God's Word. Listen to His preachers who can help you get cleaned up by challenging, comforting and enlightening you with the Holy Word of God. Consider the following: "For the word of God is alive and active. Sharper than any double-edged sword, it penetrates even to dividing soul and spirit, joints and marrow; it judges the thoughts and attitudes of the heart" (Hebrews 4:12).

When you meditate on God's Word you prosper because you are like "a tree planted by streams of water"—*living water* (see Psalm 1:3). The reason you see some trees doing better than others usually has to do with the water they are receiving. Trees need a consistent water supply even as Christians need the Word of God on a consistent basis to grow. Furthermore, the "way of the righteous" (see Psalm 1:6) includes fellowship, teaching and worship that can be found at a church that seeks after the Lord's presence and preaches His Word.

Some say that attending and serving at your local church is fruitless, but nothing can be further from the truth. You will get your best ideas in church. God can download thoughts, concepts, designs and so much more in an incredible fashion when we are in His presence! Jesus taught us that when two or three get together in the name of Jesus, His presence will begin to manifest (see Matthew 18:20). Imagine what happens when 100 people gather. Imagine when 1,000 or more get together in His Name. "Behold, how good and how pleasant it is for brethren to dwell together in unity! It is like the precious oil upon the head, running down on the beard, the beard of Aaron, running down on the edge of his garments. It is like the dew of Hermon, descending upon the mountains of Zion; for there the Lord commanded the blessing— Life forevermore" (Psalm 133:1-3, NKJV).

LAST WORD

Maybe you are like one of the three ladies at the South African restaurant who were listening in on the prayers of others… watching the actions of His people…mocking their prayers though secretly wanting someone to pray for them. Maybe sin has lured you away. Maybe you are standing at the bus stop on the pathway of sin. Whoever you are—take a tip from the thieves on the cross with Jesus. One rejected the Lord, but the other grasped the Lordship of Jesus and turned to Him to be saved. I urge you to turn your attention to the saving power of Jesus Christ and do not get caught up with the crowd of mockers, sin traffickers, and those walking in wickedness. In doing so, you will save your own soul, and everyone around you will also move toward God.

Walking, standing and sitting in sinful ways can be subtle too. Maybe you do not think of yourself as a wicked or rebellious person. Maybe you think you are religious, and that your good works alone will get you into heaven. Let's return to the story of the rich young ruler from the Gospel of Mark that I mentioned in an earlier chapter. In the account this young man hears that Jesus, the great prophet, is close by. Having been raised with a healthy respect for all the commandments, he did not want to miss the opportunity to actually speak with the amazing rabbi from Nazareth. "As Jesus started on his way, a man ran up to him and fell on his knees before him. 'Good teacher,' he asked, 'what must I do to inherit eternal life?'" (Mark 10:17).

Let me pause a minute here: did you notice that the man *ran* to Christ? For a wealthy person to run to another person was not typical for someone of his grandeur and stature! Running to another person was an act of humility; it was a genuine and earnest desire to talk with Christ. It was important to this man to speak to

Jesus in person. The young man did not care who else was around, but fell before Jesus in an act of respect and obedience.

"'Why do you call me good?' Jesus answered. 'No one is good—except God alone. You know the commandments: 'You shall not murder, you shall not commit adultery, you shall not steal, you shall not give false testimony, you shall not defraud, honor your father and mother.' 'Teacher,' he declared, 'all these I have kept since I was a boy.' Jesus looked at him and loved him." (Mark 10:18-21a).

I think when Christ looked at this young man, who was trying so desperately to do everything right, He was pleased to see that a young person (a rich one at that) had been able to keep all the commandments. Jesus was also moved by the fact that the young man was so inquisitive about ensuring his place in heaven. But that was not what made Jesus love the young man: *Christ simply loved him.*

"'One thing you lack,' He said. 'Go, sell everything you have and give to the poor, and you will have treasure in heaven. Then come, follow me.' At this the man's face fell. He went away sad, because he had great wealth" (vv. 21b-23).

The young man asked Christ what to do to be assured of eternal life, Christ told him, but he found it too costly. That is the difficulty of salvation for those who have a great deal to leave at the foot of the cross. Seldom can they be persuaded to leave it, and the cost to this man was a rich eternity with Jesus.

You cannot enter heaven with good works alone—you need to make Jesus the Lord of your life. We are all sinners...we all walk, stand and sit in the ways of sin and rebellion regardless of how we appear on the surface...rich or poor, strong or weak, young or old, famous or unknown, healthy or sick. In the end, Jesus is the only way, path, road to heaven's gate. I invite you again to pray the prayer below and truly begin living. You do not need a near-death experience as I had to find the Lord. Take God's road to eternal life:

> *We are all sinners...we all walk, stand and sit in the ways of sin and rebellion regardless of how we appear on the surface...rich or poor, strong or weak, young or old, famous or unknown, healthy or sick.*

Lord, I confess that I have had a proud heart—I have been rebellious and selfish in my ways. Forgive me. I ask You to come into my life; I ask You to change me from within. I am a sinner Lord, and I have sinned against You. Please come into my life and transform me. Be my Savior; be my Lord. Help me to seek, grow, and humble myself before You. Make me a new creation. Help me to know my purpose in Your will and to not waste the days You have given. Thank You God. Amen.

You have taken your first step! You have entered into the family of God! He will never leave you or forsake you. Grow in Him: fellowship with other believers, read His Word, and seek His counsel.

Below are six passages to nurture your growth in Him. I encourage you to commit each to memory.

- **Born Again** - "Therefore, if anyone is in Christ, the new creation has come: The old has gone, the new is here!" (2 Corinthians 5:17).

- **Study God's Word** - "How can a young person stay on the path of purity? By living according to your word" (Psalm 119:9).

- **Pray About Everything** - "Do not be anxious about anything, but in every situation, by prayer and petition, with thanksgiving, present your requests to God. And the peace of God, which transcends all understanding, will guard your hearts and your minds in Christ Jesus" (Philippians 4:6-7).

- **Fellowship with Believers** - "But encourage one another daily, as long as it is called 'Today,' so that none of you may be hardened by sin's deceitfulness" (Hebrews 3:13).

- **Share the Good News of Christ** - "Pray that I may proclaim it clearly, as I should" (Colossians 4:4).

- **Grow in God's Love** - "May the Lord direct your hearts into God's love and Christ's perseverance" (2 Thessalonians 3:5).

I am praying for you friend. I shook hands with death many years ago and nearly died. Yet, God's hand of salvation reached out and He saved me. Now, He has taken hold of you, too. God's love is amazing!

PERSONAL QUEST

1. What hinders a person from following God? (The Rich Young Ruler was reluctant because of his wealth, but each person has a stumbling block that hinders them from following the Lord.)

2. Why does the Bible strongly encourage meditating on God's Word? Isn't fellowship or praying enough?

3. How do you define "prayer" and how does it help one to walk with God?

4. When we accept God's gift of salvation we are "a new creature." Some changes happen instantly while others take time. Why?

5. What is one of your favorite verses that has helped your spiritual growth?

ABOUT THE AUTHOR

A native Texan, Mike proudly hails from West Texas. Being raised in the small town of Littlefield with five sisters and two brothers had a way of teaching him things that could never be gleaned from a textbook.

What started out with rough beginnings has blossomed into a full time ministry. Some thought he would go the way of the world but Jesus Christ stepped in when he was nineteen. Mike often quips: "I owe everything to the church. It gave me my friends, a great wife and a purpose for taking up space on the planet."

Mike earned his bachelor's degree from Southwestern Assemblies of God University. He went on to earn his Masters of Divinity from Southwestern Baptist Theological Seminary, and is pursuing his doctoral studies at Fuller Theological Seminary.

Robertson and his wife, Karen, were the pastors of Praise Temple, a church in Burleson, Texas when they received a "God Nudge" to go to Southern California. It was in Oceanside that they planted Family Fellowship Church, and were the pastors there for fifteen years.

Mike then became the Vice President of University Advancement at Southwestern Assemblies of God University (SAGU) in Waxahachie, Texas. In 2008, Mike and Karen became the lead pastors of Visalia First Assembly in Visalia, CA.

The God Nudge

One of the greatest privileges of our lives is for the God of the universe to share His heart with us. If we'll learn to listen, He'll prompt us to be involved in His work of touching lives. In this book, Pastor Mike Robertson explains the wonders and the warnings of being nudged by God. Pay attention. The concepts, stories, and applications will revolutionize your relationship with God.

I Be Jokin'...

The number one problem with public speakers today is that the attention span of the audience has been shortened. Today's culture has been so inundated with sitcoms and nine-minute content segments that after about ten minutes, you have lost them. I believe that every 30-minute speech ought to have at least half a dozen points that will make people laugh. Humor endears the audience to the speaker and makes them more receptive to what the speaker is saying.

For more information about these and other resources,
go to: www.mikedrobertson.com
Follow Mike on Twitter: @pastormikerob